SURE HIRE
Made Easy

SURE HIRE
Made Easy

Making Moves
Proven to Win the Job

Alan M. Levin

Bartleby Press

Washington • Baltimore

ISBN 978-0910155-57-1
Library of Congress Control Number: 2016937044

Portions of this edition were previously published in *Gopp, Inc. The Company that Always Gets You Hired,* by Alan M. Levin and Wayne E. Page © 1993 by Career Advancers.

Bartleby Press
PO Box 858
Savage, MD 20763
800.953.9929
BartlebythePublisher.com

Printed in the United States of America

CONTENTS

PREFACE

"It isn't what you learn that makes you successful, but what you effectively use of what you learn."— Percy H. Whiting

Job seekers, just like employers, must solve problems in order to be successful. Therefore, job seekers who learn employers' problems and show how they may provide solutions often receive offers of employment.

I believe the content matter found in *Sure Hire Made Easy* to be in concert with those who strive for excellence, who work at improving self, and who seize opportunities to build relationships.

My goal is to provide a helpful, user-friendly guide for those who must acquire in a timely fashion the job they desire. To complete this task, job seekers must remain focused and avoid distractions.

When utilized as a plan or road map, this work helps readers stay focused throughout the journey, making progress until ultimately reaching their destination. It eliminates having to explore, examine, and, then, determine if resources, third-parties, and subject matter scattered across a sprawling landscape of vast possibilities are productive. These tasks are time-consuming, distracting, and, often frustrating. It answers these basic questions; "What do I do?" and, "How do I do it?"

The text highlights activities cited most often by numerous authors and experts as most important, action parts of the job search: setting an objective, getting organized, characterizing prospective employers, arranging a daily schedule, obtaining job interviews, securing a job offer, and preserving links with others. To give the content a form easy to grasp, I've molded it into seven distinct parts: goal setting, organizing, prospecting, planning, interviewing, negotiating, and closing.

My colleagues, clients, and I refer to these elements by the acronym, Gopp, Inc.™ This format fills a void I discovered after an exhaustive examination of written and recorded materials about job search.

For readers who feel heavily constrained by time, I've included a "Jump Table" on page xiii. Select from here questions about specific areas or activities where you may need immediate answers.

While no one but you can guarantee success, I expect that job seekers who act skillfully on the principles contained in these pages are sure to get hired.

—Alan Levin

ACKNOWLEDGMENTS

I recognize and want to express gratitude to the many mentors, colleagues, clients, and friends who have helped me along the way. Some were only able to allow me a brief glimpse into their lives, but it is because of them that I've acquired the knowledge and found the inspiration to write this book. I cherish their compassion and desire to advance it by sharing my enthusiasm for this subject matter. Perhaps others may benefit from the experience I've gained over the years.

A few people provided additional support and deserve even more recognition. To them I offer my most-humble and heartfelt appreciation:

- Herschel and Rosalie Levin (of blessed memory): From you, I grew to learn about life, love, and respect. You set the standard that success requires persistence, determination, and mostly—practice.

- My darling wife, Anita: For your love, strength, inspiration, support, understanding, patience, and devotion to excellence.

- Gabrielle and Ethan: For forgiving Dad, ever-so easily, for spending too much time on less-important matters.

- My former "Pard," Wayne Emerson Page: For sharing selflessly yourself, your time, skills and knowledge. For providing for me and others direction and refinement, and doing so steadfastly with patience extraordinaire.

- My first mentors in the employment business, John Dipietro and Marvin Liebowitz. For granting me the opportunity and showing me how it's done.

- My publisher, Jeremy Kay, who exemplifies resolve and dedication to accuracy.

- My dear friend, Michael Cowan (of blessed memory): You will always be an inspiration.

- My loyal friend and "Brother," Randy Gartner; who, through fraternal love, ever-thoughtful encouragement, extraordinary talent and energy, perpetuates the outstanding.

READER'S PURPOSE

Presumably, your mission is to secure, or help someone secure, in a timely fashion, a meaningful job with a trustworthy employer. *Yes?*

Each of these "ingredients" plays an important part of successful job searching:

• Continuity of Focus • Vibrant Image • Defined Scope/Timing Component • Clarity of Voice • Convincing Demonstration of Value • Lasting Motivation • Productive Application of Efforts & Energy.

Which do you need to develop and improve? Throughout the pages that follow, identify those areas of your approach you may want to fortify. Utilize the **Gopp, Inc.**™ format as a road map or plan to…

- *Follow a proven path to your destination.* It keeps you "focused" upon your mission.

- *Eliminate chance and hope.* It helps stabilize the 'emotional roller coaster' (feelings of anticipation, disappointment, stress, frustration, and hopelessness); a common result of using impulsive approaches. Thus, it serves to protect and enhance your self image.

- *Organize and implement efficiently.* Distractions wait at every turn. When permitted to interfere, these cause the search to drag on increasing the costs. Limit diversions and you may yield success in a timely fashion, thus, condensing the search. The shorter is your search, the less costly.

- *Observe illustrations of activities which facilitate progress.* Practice and perform these to refine your message and develop a persuasive self presentation.

- *Maintain thrust.* The author is within reach, for those who desire additional support. Even the most-talented individuals sometimes find motivation in short supply.

- *Measure your progress.* Part two, Companion, includes 'paper tools' which enable you to chronicle your actions.

Equipped with *Sure Hire Made Easy*, you keep focused, boost self image, limit distractions, polish skills, stay motivated, apply efforts toward practical and attainable results and, thus, achieve your objective—To acquire, in a timely fashion, a suitable position with a reputable employer!

JUMP TABLE

Activities

Employers

Goals

Information

Interviews

Job Offers

INTRODUCTION
IT'S UP TO WHOM?

Congratulations! You hold in your hands a 'how-to' guide for conducting a successful job search; *Sure Hire Made Easy*. The activities described and illustrated herein have been field tested and proven to produce interviews and job offers among individuals seeking professional employment at all levels within the private sector. Thus, the time you invest should earn you steady progress. Consider, for a moment, a few questions employers often ask job seekers:

· Are you having difficulty getting the job you want? If yes, why?

· How many interviews have you had? Do you have any job offers? If yes, why aren't you working?

· Are you unemployed? Why did you leave your job?

· Have you ever accepted a job, and then regretted your decision?

· For what kind of job are you looking?

· Describe the right job for you.

· Why should I hire you?

HAVE YOU CONSIDERED...?

Now it's your turn. Here are a few questions you should ask:
· What's involved in conducting a successful job search?

· Am I prepared to compete with qualified job seekers for the position I want?

· Can I find reputable employers and convince them to hire me?

· How much money, time, and effort am I prepared to spend on my job search? Am I getting results? Am I under financial pressure? Feeling disappointed? Frustrated?

· How many interviews do I need to get an attractive job offer? Am I getting worthwhile interviews? Suitable offers?

· Are family and friends supporting my career plans? Am I prepared to develop new relationships to further my career?

· What's preventing me from getting the job I want?

Examine *Sure Hire Made Easy*, and discover the answers to these and other questions. Gain an understanding of the self-directed job search (SDJS), and, thus, how to secure suitable employment. Let's see how this may be accomplished.

Quick! How Do I Get A Job?

We begin with the question above, 'What's involved in conducting a successful job search?' To answer, we need first review how people usually go about finding a job.

Most often, job seekers choose "avenues of convenience" in search of employment. Let's take a ride and see where these lead.

Convenient Avenues

Job seekers who have grown attached to their computers launch the internet, where, almost magically, any topic -- including job opportunities -- appears instantaneously in digital text and graphics. Many, who have grown accustomed to seeing apparent job openings listed randomly among the 'want-ads,' casually reach for newspapers and magazines. Some job seekers, who have grown frantic, venture out to visit employment agencies and other 'referral services' setting appointments with career counselors, executive recruiters, vocational-service providers, and non-profit centers of employment assistance. And, still, others who have grown aware of 'categorized' job listings invest high hopes in 'promoters' -- paying faceless individuals and organizations typically unknown to them -- for access to these alluring 'member-only systems.'

According to publications provided by the U.S. Department of Labor, twenty percent of job seekers turn to private employment agencies. Thirty-three percent sign up with public employment services. At least sixty percent pursue advertised opportunities printed in newspapers, trade jour-

Impulsive Approaches

FOR EXPEDIENCY MANY MAKE HASTY CHOICES:

Professional employment agency
1 of every 5 sets an appointment

Federal • State employment service
1 of 3 signs up on the list

Job listings • Advertisements
6 of 10 respond

Mass mail letters • Resumes • Emails
8 of every 10 saturate the mail

nals, and other publications; some posted electronically on the internet; and, more aired on television and radio.[1] As many as eighty percent of those seeking employment send to prospective employers unsolicited letters, resumes, and emails.[2]

Researchers, independents and those connected with the Department of Labor, periodically conduct studies about employment and the job market. They've found that most people among the civilian (non-military) labor force, who find they must search for employment, choose paths of convenience. Fact is, these approaches are expensive and time-consuming, and, thus, the resulting searches prove costly and lengthy.

• Employment Agencies & Services, E- and Snail Mail

Though they help find jobs for a number of job seekers, professional employment agencies and placement specialists fail most job seekers who use them. The average placement rate for employment agencies is five percent.[3] The U.S. employment service and state employment offices place one of every six persons who use them. Fifty percent of those who get jobs this way are back looking again before thirty days or less.[4] Almost all who email and mail resumes in response to advertisements fail to get hired this way. Advertisements produce large numbers of responses. Usually, one-hundred responses produce only two to five interviews. Job seekers who respond to ads, routinely overlook the importance of investigating the job and whether it is suitable for them. Often, those who do get hired wind up mismatched and employed in short-lived jobs.[5]

Every day, employers receive numerous unsolicited emails, resumes, cover letters, and broadcast letters. While a few job seekers do get hired this way (two to three percent of employers respond), qualifications and experience in print provide employers a measure to disqualify candidates. Others may, and often do, match or exceed your qualifications and experience. The employer's perception of

Bet on These Odds?	
Job-search method	**Success rate**
Private employment agency	5%
Public employment service	0-10%
Respond to ads	5%
Mass mailings	3%

you as a personality is more important.[6] Let's consider the efficacy of a few other popular methods of job searching.

• Placement Offices, Job Fairs, and Advertising

College graduates sometimes use the school placement office to seek employment opportunities. One of ten succeeds in getting a job this way.[7] Some job seekers go to places where employers come to hire, job fairs, for example. Of those who try this method, eight in a hundred succeed.[8] Others advertise themselves through unsolicited print and videos. Like sending unsolicited resumes, this approach yields an interview two or three percent of the time. Less than one percent of jobs are secured this way.[9]

More Impulsive Efforts

Job-search method	Success rate
School placement offices	10%
Job fairs	8%
Self-placed ads • videos	1%

• Third-Party Assistance: Help or Hindrance?

All these approaches to finding jobs share a common factor: Dependence. To advance, job seekers depend on intermediaries or "third parties" to act in a helpful and fruitful manner.

Those who conduct searches using these approaches relinquish control. Success depends upon a contribution requiring effort from someone else (typically a stranger). For many job seekers, third parties are costly. In most cases they never deliver, leaving job seekers in suspense; impeding progress. Job seekers spend substantial energy, time, and money only to wind up frustrated and discouraged. They may convey these feelings to employers who are, of course, reluctant to hire them. When they do succeed, all too often, the opportunities are unsuitable. Consequently, their job searches drag on, and their careers remain disrupted.

These avenues of convenience lead job seekers to wander aimlessly around

What of Relying on Others?
With control in hands of others:
Job searches prove lengthy • Costly
Job seekers often frustrated • Take meager jobs

their intended destination. Lost from sight is the importance of developing a results-oriented, job-search plan. Other factors, too, play a role in searching for a job.

External Factors

Variables affecting employers (those who provide job opportunities), like budget restraints, impact the job search. These 'factors,' may take the form of structural changes in the economy, i.e. emerging technologies (requiring specialized training), fluctuating interest rates, inflation, rates of growth of various market segments, make-up of the population, and changing global conditions. While remaining outside the control of any individual, these are 'external.' Job seekers take aim at rapid success when they anticipate and allow for external factors.

The U.S. Department of Labor conducts studies and projects trends of the American economy. Their findings are posted online at www.bls.gov. The current population survey is updated monthly. Other publications are published periodically, such as the Report on the American Workforce. These demographics are important, whether you're looking for work, already have a job, or are considering a change. They're indicators of your value to employers. Here are some highlights.

• Education

The majority of 21st century jobs require education and training beyond high school. In 2006, there were more than two times as many college-educated individuals in the work place over age twenty-five as in 1970. By 2010, those having less than a high-school education held only eight percent of all jobs.

> *College is Popular*
> **In 2006, 61% new jobs require:**
> Education beyond high school

Also important to note, since 1970, rates of unemployment are lowest among those with four years or more of college.[10]

• Skills

Professional employment requires advanced-level abilities. For businesses to survive in a highly-competitive global economy, employees must communicate with proficiency, solve complex problems, and, more than ever, ably work together with others.

Increasingly, employers are hiring individuals with exceptional literacy, communication, language, and computational skills.[11]

In 2007, there were approximately 153 million people in the civilian work force. By 2018,

> *Highly-Skilled Need Apply*
> **Employers seek candidates w/:**
> Verbal communication skills
> Speak multiple languages • Writing
> Basic • Advanced computer • Math
> Analytical • Problem solving • Teamwork

- **21st-Century Jobs Require Intermediate & Highly-Advanced Skills**

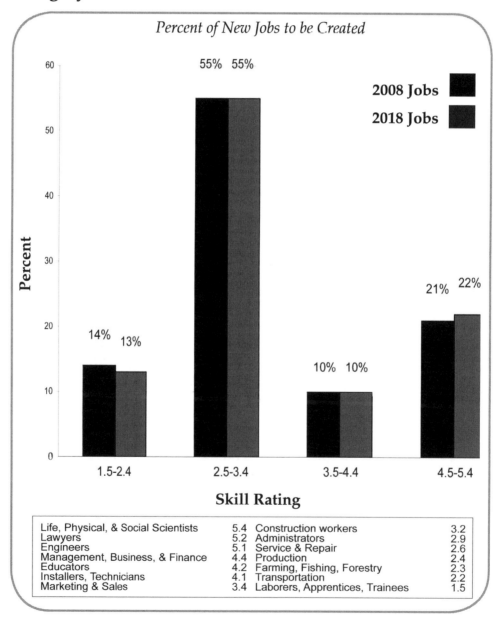

Percent of New Jobs to be Created

2008 Jobs
2018 Jobs

Life, Physical, & Social Scientists	5.4	Construction workers	3.2
Lawyers	5.2	Administrators	2.9
Engineers	5.1	Service & Repair	2.6
Management, Business, & Finance	4.4	Production	2.4
Educators	4.2	Farming, Fishing, Forestry	2.3
Installers, Technicians	4.1	Transportation	2.2
Marketing & Sales	3.4	Laborers, Apprentices, Trainees	1.5

estimates project this number to reach 166 million. Women, minorities, and immigrants account for ninety percent of this anticipated growth.

• Gender

Numbers of women entering the labor force continue to increase. In 2006, more than 70 million women, age sixteen and over comprised forty-six percent. Though men continue to dominate the work force, through 2018, the number of working women grows closer to equal the number of men (as their numbers are predicted to decline). Source: bls

• Age

Oddly, from 2008 through 2018 numbers of those between the ages of sixteen and twenty-four are estimated to decline by 1.5 million. Workers between twenty-five and fifty-four, though the largest portion of the labor force, will also undergo a reduction in number. It's expected, however, that the number of workers fifty-five and over intensifies by 11 million! Come 2018, almost a quarter of the faces in the workplace will belong to those born during and shortly after the baby-boom generation (see plate, pg. 8).

As the number of middle-aged workers increases, competition intensifies for middle-management positions. Thus, many middle-aged job seekers become less attractive to employers. Moreover, full-time work schedules and employer-provided benefits; such as annual raises, health-care contracts and other insurance, are likely to change.[12]

• Age and the Job Search

Generally, the older is the job seeker, the longer the search. For those between twenty and twenty-four, the average length of time between jobs (last studied in 2007) is 15.3 weeks. For those between thirty-five and forty-four, it's 18.7 weeks. Job seekers between fifty-five and sixty-four take an average of 22.2 weeks to get re-employed, nearly one-and-a-half times as long as their youngest counterparts.[13]

• The Service Sector

The service industries collect, manipulate, and

Veterans of Business Take Longer	
Age	Average length of search
20-24	15.3 weeks
35-44	18.7 weeks
55-64	22.2 weeks

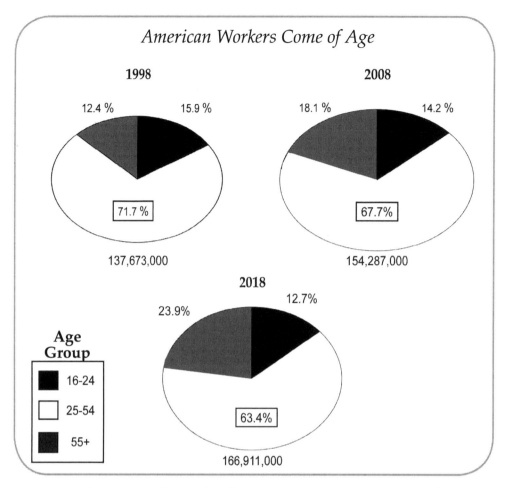

American Workers Come of Age

1998

12.4 %   15.9 %

71.7 %

137,673,000

2008

18.1 %   14.2 %

67.7%

154,287,000

2018

23.9%   12.7%

63.4%

166,911,000

Age Group

- ■ 16-24
- □ 25-54
- ■ 55+

process information. These businesses create value by providing services without manufacturing tangible products. The service industries continue to experience strong demand for talent. Ninety percent of the net increase of jobs over the next ten years is anticipated to occur in the service sector.

By 2016, non-farm wage and salary employment in the service sector is predicted to approach eighty-five percent of the workforce.[14]

• New Jobs by Industry

The chart that follows lists industries which are expected to generate large numbers of new jobs during the ten-year period through 2018.[15] Notice

Of Non-Farm Employment

80% in the service sector

Wholesale • Retail trade
Education • Information
Hospitality • Food service
Health
Public administration
Finance • Insurance • Real estate
Transportation
Public utilities
Business • Trade services

that most are service-related industries. (For expanded list, see: http://www.bls.gov/emp/ep_table_204.htm).

Areas of New Jobs Through 2018

Industry	2008 Jobs	2018 Jobs	Industry	2008 Jobs	2018 Jobs
Retail • Grocery Stores	15,356	16,010	Nursing • Personal-Care Facilities	3,008	3,645
Eating • Drinking Places	9,632	10,371	Machinery • Equipment Wholesalers	5,964	6,220
New • Repair Construction	7,215	8,552	Computer • Data Process-ing Services	1,450	2,107
Offices of Health Practitioners	3,713	4,977	Home Health Care	958	1,399
Personnel-supply Services	3,144	3,744			

(In Thousands)

• Occupations with Largest Job Growth

Here are some of the occupations projected to produce the most hires during the decade from 2008-2018.[16]

Estimated New Jobs Over Ten Years

Category Class	Number 2008	Estimated 2018	Category Class	Number 2008	Estimated 2018
Salespersons (Retail)	4,489	4,863	Truck-Drivers (Light • Heavy)	1,798	2,031
General Office Clerks	3,024	3,381	Postsecondary Teachers	1,699	1,956
Food Counter (Prep • Service Workers)	2,701	3,096	Nurses Aides	1,469	1,745
Registered Nurses	2,618	3,200	Janitors • Maintenance	1,361	1,509
Waiters • Waitresses	2,381	2,533	Receptionists • Info Clerks	1,139	1,312
Customer-Service Representatives	2,252	2,651	Home-Health Aides	921	1,382
			Personal • Home-Care Aides	817	1,193

(In Thousands)

A Self-Directed Job Search?

We examined popular approaches taken by job seekers: Such methods as sending emails, resumes, and letters. Tactics like going to exployment agencies, placement centers and job fairs. Impulsive choices like these require reliance on third parties. Job seekers must depend on others to act; relinquishing control and, incorporating hope and chance into their formula for success. We mentioned that external factors, such as the changing economy, impact the search. Like the popular practices, external factors remain beyond the control of the job seeker. Therefore, to focus upon getting hired quickly, job seekers need employ activities which they may control; and, choose a realistic target by anticipating and allowing for those external factors likely to impact their search.

Now, let's return to our ride. When job seekers take the initiative to locate and secure employment, and assume control of the process, theirs becomes a self-directed job search (SDJS). This strategy involves a plan, which includes organizing and executing the search from start to finish. For some, this may be compared to "taking the wheel," and having to navigate the entire way to their destination. To prepare for launching a SDJS, begin down the road of responsibility and initiative by examining these questions (answers to follow).

· How often does the average person change jobs?

· Of all jobs how many are advertised?

· Which criteria do employers use to assess job seekers?

· Why do many job seekers remain unemployed longer than they expect?

· Which are the most successful ways to find jobs?

• How Often Do We Change Jobs?

The average American worker changes jobs frequently. Those under the age of thirty-five switch jobs every fifteen months. If you're over thirty-five, you belong with those who change on average every five years.[17]

> *Job Changes*
> **Under age 35**
> Every 1.25 years
> **Over age 35**
> Every 5 years

Many careers, therefore, involve a number of job searches. If you fit the statistical average, you may wind up having twelve to sixteen jobs during your career.

• Percent of Advertised Jobs?

Advertised jobs open or broadcast to the public (described and/or listed in print, on TV, radio, and internet), represent fifteen to twenty percent of all jobs available at any given time. The other eighty to eighty-five percent are "hidden" from view. These jobs, unadvertised, are known to employers, employees, and "insiders." Clearly, most job opportunities remain shielded within the borders of the "hidden job market."[18]

> **Most Jobs Concealed from Public**
> **15-20% jobs**
> Advertised • Broadcast • Listed
> **80-85% jobs**
> Unpublicized • Hidden from public

• How Employers Evaluate Job Seekers?

Employers screen job seekers by assessing three criteria: appearance, dependability, and skills. Appearance refers to the impression given the employer by the job seeker via: paper (in print), on a monitor screen (electronic file, video feed), voice (audio message), and, in person (live, face to face).

If you pass the appearance test, employers next judge your trustworthiness: Are you on time? Can you be depended upon to produce? Are you a team player?

If you pass these two tests, employers will then assess your skills. Is your background and experience valuable to the employer? If no, can you be trained?

> **Employers Assess Candidate Appeal in Three Areas**
> **Appearance(s)**
> Resume • Letter • E-file
> Phone call • Video conference
> Recording • Face-to-face
> **Dependability**
> Punctual • Productive
> Work w/ others
> **Skills**
> Relevant • Trainable

Interestingly, more job seekers are eliminated from consideration because they flunk the "appearance" criterion, even though they may possess the skills to do the job.[19]

• Why do Job Seekers Remain Unemployed?

Problems with communication are most common among job seekers. Often, those who get rejected by employers do so because they fail to communicate effectively. In general, they're unprepared for the job search. Examples include: unexciting or unacceptable image, failing to clearly identify and describe strengths and accomplishments, and; giving unclear, unimaginative, unrelated, unrealistic, or unbelievable answers to interview questions. These problems are compounded for those job seekers who have a vague understanding of the job market, and who spend too little time looking for a job.[20]

Many Sincere Job Seekers Fail to get Offers

Of all job seekers	Reason for lengthy job search
40%	Unacceptable appearance
80%	Unable to convey skills
80%	Flunk the interview
90%	Improvise fruitlessly
98%	Commit too little time

• Which are the Productive Ways to Find Jobs?

Two activities; networking, and approaching employers directly, consistently yield the highest number of job offers. Using these methods, approximately seventy-five percent of professionals, technicians, and managers get hired. Networking, finding job opportunities by tapping into relatives, friends, and acquaintances; accounts for nearly forty percent of all hires. About one-third of job seekers who get hired approach employers directly.[21] Both of these activities may be planned, performed, and controlled by the job seeker.

Gainful Approaches

Method	Percent jobs obtained
Networking	40%
Direct contact w/ employers	35%

Benefiting from the SDJS

A SDJS begins as the job seeker climbs into the driver's seat and assumes complete charge. S/he proceeds to plan, organize, practice, perform, chronicle and evaluate activities which produce job offers. Now, you may be wondering; should I go ahead and attempt to control my job search entirely? Answer: Of course.

When you implement a SDJS, you may determine how to measure and adjust the pace of your progress, protect and enhance your self image, hone skills, and, consequently; acquire a suitable job in a timely fashion. Here's how:

- *Efficient application of efforts & energy.* By taking actions which you control, i.e. *initiating conversations about your job search*; you may minimize distractions, diversions, and chance. Such actions enable you to yield results in an orderly and timely fashion, thus condensing the search. The shorter it lasts the less it costs.

- *Vibrant image.* You advance your progress without having to rely and wait on others to act, guess, or hope that things happen. Acting on your own behalf protects you from feelings of anticipation, stress, frustration, and hopelessness (common results of using impulsive approaches). As your efforts are gainful, your confidence grows. Able to impart a spellbinding image, the result of enhanced composure, helps you win interviews and offers.

- *Persuasive self presentation.* As you implement your SDJS, you read, write, observe and speak. These skills are required in many jobs. When proficient at them, you communicate effectively and, thus, make a dynamic impression upon others.

> ### *Benefits of Taking Charge*
> **To implement ably self-directed activities:**
> Focus upon actions under your control
> Protects & enhances self-image
> Improves communication skills • Grows Confidence
> Wins interviews & offers
> Helps condense search • Contain costs
> Secure suitable job • Advances career

The SDJS enables you to affect your progress, image, skills, secure a meaningful job, advancing your career all, in a timely and cost-effective manner. Are you prepared to accept full responsibility for shaping and promoting your business or professional image and, ultimately, your success?

SEVEN STEPS TO SUCCESSFUL SDJS

In *Sure Hire Made Easy*, I've attempted to explain how job seekers may control the job search. The content printed upon these pages serves as a guide for the journey to a suitable offer of employment. Here's a thumbnail sketch of the SDJS plan:

Step one; *Goal Setting*. Here, job seekers begin by setting a clear goal. Careful attention to choosing a realistic objective results with a self description, a job title, and a job description.

Continue by *Organizing* the search. Devise a system to keep accurate records of relevant information and activities.

Next; *Prospecting*. Identify reputable employers who may be interested in hiring you. Two productive ways to do this: reading and networking.

In the fourth step; *Planning*, job seekers make ready to interact confidently with persons who hire. To persuade employers to grant an interview requires a solid understanding of skills, a convincing presentation of self, and productive execution of daily activities.

Interviewing; step five, is where job offers materialize. To convince employers of one's value, however, requires conscientious preparation, an inspired performance, and a thorough evaluation of each interview.

Offers of employment may be accepted as offered, enhanced, or rejected. Step six; *Negotiating*, is where a mutually-beneficial agreement is shaped. Job seekers may find it helpful to define needs, and review a written proposal. Then they may make an informed decision whether to begin a new job.

Step seven is *Closing*. The book concludes by examining this important activity. The basic principle of 'closing' is simple: Ask and you shall receive. Want information? Ask for it. Want to meet an employer? Ask to meet. Want a job? Ask for one!

Memorize the steps of the self-directed job search. Imagine a corporation with a fine reputation has issued you an assignment. Your task: To confirm the location of an employer alleged to operate among a vast array of business enterprises. You must undertake a journey to

Seven Steps of SDJS

Gopp, Inc.™:
Goal Setting
Organizing
Prospecting
Planning
Interviewing
Negotiating

prove this hypothetical employer actually exists. Clearly, you need to determine a correct course, depart, guide your progress, and arrive to positively identify this theoretical employer. Accomplish this mission by implementing successfully a seven-part plan. Thus, the job-search adventure begins.

What's the name of this imaginary corporation? It's "Gopp, Inc."™ Each letter represents a step toward a sure hire (your destination): **G**oal Setting, **O**rganizing, **P**rospecting, **P**lanning, **I**nterviewing, **N**egotiating, and **C**losing. Simply put, job seekers who complete the seven steps find themselves suitably employed.

Key Terms and Concepts

As you read through the material, note that key terms and concepts stand out prominently. *Italics* highlight *key terms, phrases,* and *concepts.* Words printed in ***bold italics*** (found in the body text) are preceded or followed by definitions.

Mary Emerson is a fictional character. Mary serves to illustrate a self-directed job seeker. One whom has assumed control of the job search. She's a member of an elite group of job seekers. Five to ten percent of those among the job-seeking population assume control of their destiny. [22] Contained in the text are boxes that feature a drop shadow. These illustrate forms Mary used to advance her progress (for sample, see: step one, *Goal Setting*, Mary Emerson's Personal Assessment). Part Two of this book; Companion, contains sample blank forms which readers may utilize for the job search.

The ***employer*** is an organization, corporation, company, business, or key individual. Employers hire and compensate people (employ-

Key Terms are Easy to Discern
Italics **highlight:**
Key terms • Phrases • Concepts
***Bold italics* identify terms which are defined:**

Mary Emerson
Fictional character
Self-directed job seeker
Represents 5-10% of job seekers

Employer
Organization • Company • Individual
Hires • Compensates workers
Exchange for labor

4-step formula
Attention-grabber
Identify
Payoff
Signoff

Self-directed job search (SDJS)
Planned strategy • Activities performed
Controlled by job seekers
Aim to locate • Secure suitable employment

ees) in exchange for labor or services. Reputable employers seek long-term relationships with employees secured by legal means adhering strictly to applicable state, federal and local laws.

You'll find a **four-step formula** to follow when making telephone calls, writing letters of reference, interviewing, and when negotiating. The first step is the *Attention-Grabber.* To begin a productive exchange with a person, arouse her/his interest and/or secure (ask for) a commitment. The second step is *Identify.* Here, establish the groundwork for productive communications: describe yourself, establish a connection, and summarize relevant, prior activities. In step three; *Payoff,* you request or supply information to help build rapport. Finally, as you *Signoff,* display proper courtesy, and express intent to follow up.

SUMMARY

Many business people manage closely their schedule reporting reliably to their job each day, yet, devote little, if any, time to managing their career. Often they're surprised when, just as they've settled into a routine and all seems stable, they unexpectedly lose their job. As job seekers, they're unprepared for the search ahead.

Most job seekers embark -- to gain entrance, or re-enter into the world of employment -- having to navigate without a plan. They choose 'convenient avenues' (i.e. launching the web, circulating resumes, meeting agents, investing in promoters), placing control of their careers in the hands of others, hoping that job offers happen to come along. They may disregard factors outside their immediate control ('external') which play a role in the job search. For example: education, skills, gender, age, the ever-changing demand for talent within the market, structural changes in the economy, and types of jobs available. Such job searches are often lengthy and costly. Many accept offers only to be at the search again soon after. This process diverts job seekers, leading them aimlessly on an 'emotional roller coaster,' around their intended destination; producing disappointment, stress, frustration, and feelings of hopelessness.

The **self-directed job search (SDJS)** is a strategy undertaken to acquire suitable employment which puts the job seeker in complete control of the process. It makes use of selected activities, proven to produce results. Through SDJS activities, described and illustrated in this book, readers learn ways to find, meet, and impress employers who routinely screen untrained and unprepared job seekers. When they utilize this seven-step plan, Gopp, Inc.™ job seekers organize and implement without having to wait on others, guess, or hope. Given careful attention and skillful performance of the activities, success may be achieved in a timely and cost-effective manner.

Sure Hire Made Easy keeps readers focused upon making progress and completing their mission. It helps limit distractions, thus, condense the search. Examine the Gopp, Inc.™ map to grasp in the mind's eye, the adventure ahead of you. Follow it and put the search under your control. These seven steps; *Goal Setting, Organizing, Prospecting, Planning, Interviewing, Negotiating, and Closing*, make easy the journey to a sure hire. Continue down the road to success. Your project begins with *Goal Setting.*

1. GOAL SETTING

ESTABLISHING THE TARGET

IN THIS CHAPTER...

Determine or re-examine your professional identity:

- *Compose a self-description. It's your key for "unlocking the doors" to contacts, employers, and others.*
- *Choose a suitable job title.*
- *Form a description of the job you want.*

So, you're looking for a job. A friend introduces you to an employer for whom you think you'd really like to work. Wow! That's great! Until, the employer says, "Tell me, Who are you?, What do you do?, and What do you think this job involves?" Can you answer these questions without hesitation?

Expect employers to ask these basic questions and others like them. When you prepare clear and concise answers to these three questions, you establish your job-search goal.

THIS WAY TO WORK!

Goal setting is a process of establishing a professional or occupational identity. Complete the first step of the Gopp, Inc.™ project, by setting a goal. The care you take in doing this affects the efficiency and, eventually, the overall success of your job search. The clearer your goal, the easier to communicate it to others.

To set your goal, first clarify in your mind who you are by writing a clear self description (Who are you?). Next, decide what you do, or, want to do, by choosing an appropriate job title. Then, define the duties you'll perform by writing an accurate job description (What the job involves).

> *Goal Setting*
> **Process to Establish Professional Identity**
> **3 Aspects of Goal Setting:**
> SELF DESCRIPTION—*Who You Are*
> JOB TITLE—*What You Do*
> JOB DESCRIPTION—*What the Job Requires*

Who Are You?

A *self description* is a one-paragraph summary of a person's experiences and abilities. When you share your self description with someone, you describe yourself in thirty seconds or less. In the process, you project a self-confident, professional image.

How should you prepare a self description? Begin with a personal assessment. Let's see how Mary Emerson composed her self description. She began by writing answers to the personal-assessment questions. (Part two, Companion, *Self-Description Project*.)

• Mary Emerson's Personal Assessment

1. Name the last three jobs you've held. Give dates. (Begin with the most recent job. Include paid, volunteer, or informal work, home activities, military duties, or work-study experiences.)

   Graphic Artist/Publicist, Media Services Department, Grayson Corporation, 6/15/-- to 3/9/--. Multimedia Editor, University of Maryland's "Diamondback," Public Relations Department, 1/10/-- to 6/3/--.

2. What special knowledge and skills (developed abilities; things you do well) do you possess that an employer might find valuable? The skills may include job-related skills, or skills you can transfer to a new job.

   Speak and write well
   Taught novices to use PC Paintbrush
   Saved employer money by learning to desk-top publish
   Develop and organize advertising promos
   Generate computer graphics with CAD program
   Edit news releases, campus newspaper
   Thorough researcher and organizer
   Connect with various types of people

3. List your credentials, degrees, awards, licenses, evidence of education, and special training. Name professional or amateur affiliations.

BA in Communication Arts, University of Maryland
Goucher Award for Creative Graphics
Member of the American Marketing Association

4. Describe briefly your interests and hobbies that may be of interest to employers.

Enjoy creating cartoons, fantasy characters
I like reading Spanish and Italian
Like to discuss graphic art with friends and acquaintances
Like varied work schedule

5. Name the job/position you're most interested in obtaining. If you cannot name a job, name a career field. (If unsure, write "undecided.")

Sales Rep. in Media Arts (or) Advertising Field

Finish the personal assessment. Use it to write a self description. It should take very little time and effort. Write it, learn it, and practice delivering it orally. Enable yourself to communicate clearly your self description in a few moments.

To prepare her self description, Mary Emerson drew on information from her personal assessment. Her self description is a five-sentence summary derived from her inventory. The following is her completed self-description inventory.

• Mary's Self-Description Inventory

Length of Work/Special Knowledge and Skills

I worked in media services for two years at the Grayson Corporation. I worked one year editing text and graphics for the "Diamondback," at the University of Maryland. I've generated computer graphics and created line art for publication. I've also conducted research and written news and ad copy.

Education, Special Training, Credentials
(Affiliations, Awards, Certificates, Licenses)

I have a BA in Communication Arts and have received the Goucher Award for creative graphics. I am presently a member of the American Marketing Association.

Interests and Hobbies

I like to create illustrations and draw cartoons. When I have time, I read books written in Spanish and Italian. I enjoy learning new technology and keeping up to date with the latest developments in the advertising field. I'm interested in a job that offers a flexible schedule and a variety of activities.

Self Description

I've been in the advertising field for three years researching, creating, and composing various print and video projects. I write, edit, design and produce camera-ready artwork on the computer. I have a BA in Communication Arts and received the Goucher Award for creative graphics. I'm a member of the American Marketing Association. I've organized discussions among arts-and-graphics professionals to learn more about the advertising industry.

• Why Compose a Self Description?

When job seekers share a self description, they tell others 'who' they are. The *self description* is a key to a successful job search.

Use it when you introduce yourself to contacts, colleagues, and prospective employers. Keep it clear and concise. The self description is illustrated, later, when we examine networking (step three, *Prospecting*), initial communications with employers (step four, *Planning*), and the job-summary card (step seven, *Closing*).

> *Key to Successful Job Searching*
> **Use Self Description:**
> When you meet others
> During telephone & online conversations
> When corresponding

What's Your Job?

Let's answer the employer's second question, "What do you do?" This question usually means; What is your profession (occupation or job)? The answer you give, say, "administrative aide," "software engineer," "retail store manager," is your job title.

A *job title* is a generic name, tag, or 'label' which signifies the type of work one performs. It may comprise a single, couple, or a few word(s) and specify a functional part (department or location) within an organization. Also, it may denote the level of one's corporate responsibility or authority. Boxes depicted as parts of an organizational chart, which links positions in a hierarchical fashion, feature such names or labels. If you have a job, you probably have a job title.

As a job seeker, you need a job title, too. People identify you by what you do. Employers identify with you, and will consider hiring you, when they're convinced you know what you do. Do you need to identify, revise, or update your job title? Now may be a good time to review it to determine how accurately it reflects what you actually do (or prefer to do).

If you don't have one, how do you ascertain a job title? To select a realistic job title demands careful thought and introspection. Anticipate and allow for those external factors likely to impact your search. (*Introduction*, External Factors.) You may need to do some research.

> *Job Title*
> **A Label For What You Do:**
> *Marketing Representative*
> *Senior Account Executive*
> *Project Manager*

• Selecting a Job Title

Find occupational and career guides online. Or, at the library locate the career-resource section. Find the *Career Guide to Industries* (CGI), U.S. Dept. of Labor, Labor Statistics Bureau, Bulletin 2701, latest edition. The "CGI" cross references job titles and job skills.[23]

The O*NET® (Occupational Information Network) is a database of job or occupational titles compiled by the Department of Labor. It supersedes the seventy-year-old *Dictionary of Occupational Titles* (last published in 1991). It links more than 900 job titles to various descriptors including skills, abilities, knowledge, tasks, work activities, work context, experience levels required, job interests, work values/needs and work styles. Each title is listed under an O*NET-SOC (standard occupational classification) eight-digit code. Updated twice annually, it continues to undergo periodic enhancements. Portions of this information are printed by various publishers and available in book form among the career-resource section at public and college libraries. Available online with the database, the O*NET® provides Career Exploration Tools (Interest Profiler) designed to help users identify job types. Access O*NET® online. [24]

The "OOH" (*Occupational Outlook Handbook*, U.S. Dept. of Labor, Labor Statistics Bureau, Bulletin 2700) lists forecasts, job descriptions, training requirements, salaries, and work conditions of hundreds of occupations accounting for about seven of every eight jobs in the United States. Revised every two years. (To locate specific jobs, use the index in the back of the Handbook.) [25]

Career Guides

CGI
Jobs by interest areas
Titles listed alphabetically

O*NET® Online
900 Titles / Descriptions

OOH
Job descriptions
Qualifications
Job-market forecasts

JIST PUBLISHING CATALOGUE
Guides to title selection

PEOPLE IN YOUR CAREER FIELD
Ask for their titles
Ask about others' titles

TAKE CAREER INTEREST TESTS-"CDM-R"

In addition to these career indexes, there are many helpful resources to investigate when choosing a suitable job title.

JIST Publishing, Indianapolis, Indiana, has an extensive catalogue for job seekers which contains numerous guides to job-title selection. Contact people in your career field. Ask them to tell you the job titles of employees who do the kind of work you're interested in doing.

If you need additional guidance, the "CDM-R" (*Career Decision Making System, Revised*), a self-scoring, career-interest test, may be helpful.[26] For other career-interest tests, google and contact companies that specialize in self-assessment instruments. Let's see how Mary Emerson did with her job-title choices:

• Mary's Job-Title Choices

Mary found three likely job titles, "Graphic Designer," "Art Director," and "Advertising Sales Agent," listed on O*Net® online in the 'Code Connector' section. Her first choice, located at code 41-3011.00, "*Advertising Sales Agent*." It's a practical match in light of her interests, education, and work values. Also, it's a close fit to her life-and-work experience and to her skills.

> *Mary's Choices Reflect*
> **Her Interests and Skills**
> Graphic Designer
> Art Director
> Advertising Sales Agent

What's Your Job Involve?

The last part of *Goal setting* is to form an accurate description of the job. Employers expect job seekers to have a basic understanding of the duties and responsibilities of the job they're seeking. Often, employers ask: "If I hire you, what do you think your responsibilities would be?" How can you describe your responsibilities to a prospective employer, one who has yet to hire you?

A **job description** summarizes briefly the responsibilities and duties of a particular job. Here's how to get information about a job you may want.

> *Job Description*
> **Summary of Job Responsibilities • Duties**
> Know your job description
> Employers seek those who know what their job entails
> Indicates you've done your homework

• Writing the Job Description

Go to the O*Net® online. Here, summary reports are available for each job title by SOC code number. Under 'tasks,' general job duties are listed. Also, look for 'work activities' or responsibilities. If more information is needed, check out the Occupational Outlook Handbook.

Locate and contact professionals in the career field who have your job title. Ask them to summarize their day-to-day activities. These "industry contacts" provide checks against dated or irrelevant information. They may give you a current overview of the industry and the status of any changes taking place.

Write a job description and make it your own. Copy the job description with job title(s) from the O*Net®. Include related information from the OOH and from what professionals in your career field have told you. Summarize the responsibilities and duties in four or five sentences.

Find Sample Job Descriptions
OCCUPATIONAL INFORMATION NETWORK (O*NET®)
Titles and Job Descriptions
OCCUPATIONAL OUTLOOK HANDBOOK (OOH)
Career-Field Descriptions
CONTACT PEOPLE IN YOUR CAREER FIELD
Ask About Duties

Mary Emerson's job description is a distillation of O*Net®-SOC code number 41-3011.00 and input from talking with professionals working in this job. It's brief (only four sentences), to the point, and it answers the question, "What do you think this job involves?"

• Mary Emerson's Job Description:

*I'll call on advertising agencies, manufacturers, and other businesses needing graphic-art services, such as layout, illustration, and photography. I'll advise customers in methods of composing layouts. I'll inform customers of types of art work available through this company. I'll compute job costs and deliver advertising or illustration proofs to customers for approval and purchase. (Partial-source: summary report for O*Net®-SOC 41-3011.00)*

When you compose a self description, select a job title, and write a job description, you've set your job-search goal. Here's Mary Emerson's goal:

Mary Emerson's Professional Identity

Write A Self Description

I've been in the advertising field for three years researching, creating, and composing various print and video projects. I write, edit, design and produce camera-ready artwork on the computer. I have a BA in Communication Arts and received the Goucher Award for creative graphics. I'm a member of the American Marketing Association. I've organized discussions among arts-and-graphics professionals to learn more about the advertising industry.

Write Your Job Title

Advertising Sales Agent

Write Your Job Description

I'll call on advertising agencies, manufacturers, and other businesses needing graphic-art services, such as layout, illustration, and photography. I'll advise customers in methods of composing layouts. I'll inform customers of types of art work available through this company. I'll compute job costs and deliver advertising or illustration proofs to customers for approval and purchase.

SUMMARY

Goal setting is the first step of the Gopp, Inc.™ project. Job seekers successfully launch the SDJS by establishing a clear goal. Employers are busy people who have little time for job seekers unsure of their occupational or job goals. Directness and a no-nonsense approach is the rule when interacting with prospective employers.

Earlier, we introduced goal setting by placing the job seeker in a hypothetical situation engaged in a cursory conversation with an employer who asks, "Who are you?," "What do you do?," and "What do you think this job involves?"

Prepare precise responses to these questions. Job seekers who do, distinguish themselves. Employers are often deluged with requests from individuals who have only vague notions of what they want. Goal setting helps job seekers define their (desired) position in the work place, and it clarifies the nature of the opportunity they seek.

When job seekers clearly articulate knowledge of these basic matters, they convey to others that they're knowledgeable, prepared, and goal-oriented.

Three things comprise a realistic job-search goal: First, a *self description* based on a personal assessment. This is a short, one-paragraph summary of experiences and skills. Use it when networking (step three, *Prospecting*) and when initiating interaction with employers (step four, *Planning*). It answers the question, "Who are you?"

Second, a *job title*: A single- or multiple-word tag or label for the type of work the job seeker does or wants to do. Respond to the question, "What do you do?" with your job title.

Third, a *job description*: A concise breakdown of the general requirements of the job. A clear, concise response to an employer who asks, "What do you think this job entails?" gives the job seeker credibility. It distinguishes serious job seekers from those unprepared to accurately answer such questions.

With a clearly-defined goal, the job seeker has established the target. Next, proceed to step two.

2. ORGANIZING
MANAGING INFORMATION

IN THIS CHAPTER...

Obtain and arrange tools necessary to track your progress:

- *Assemble means to manage and record activities which yield interviews and offers.*

- *Position files to sort and store information.*

Step two in the Gopp, Inc.™ project, **Organizing**, begins as the job seeker assembles tools to guide and measure progress. To succeed at job searching, job seekers often need record pertinent information, and; they must manage and perform in a skillful and effective manner, activities which yield results. This requires thorough note making. So, select a desk in a place free from distractions. Furnish with note-making materials, computer, telephone, calendar, digital or cassette recorder with tapes, and inexpensive telephone pick-up (microphone). Prepare to gather a suitable personal-information-manager application, file folders, index cards, blank forms and logs. Let's define some key terms associated with measuring the job search.

MEASURES OF THE SEARCH

A **lead** (pronounced, "leed") is an employer (company, corporation, organization, business, or key person) with a pressing need to fill a job opening, or the foresight to implement a policy of creating a new position whenever advantageous, and; able to make a hire intended to initiate a long-term association. Job seekers and others refer to such employer by the name of the company, corporation, organization, or business.

Remember these five points about *leads*:

- Identified by the name of the company, corporation, organization, or business

- Fixing a need by hiring someone to fill a job opening

- Creating a new position spontaneously to fulfill company policy

• Able to act now

• Intent upon initiating a long-term association.

Since all companies must acquire new talent to survive and grow, virtually all successful companies symbolize *leads*. It's the job seeker however, who must identify those select few companies most fit to gain by hiring her/him. (In step three, *Prospecting*, we discuss how job seekers may accomplish this.)

A **contact** is an individual who provides names, and information about people and companies, helping facilitate the job seeker's progress.

Actions job seekers perform intended to secure job interviews and offers are **primary activities**. For example: speaking and corresponding with contacts and employers. **Support activities**, for example: jaunts to purchase search-related materials and supplies, supplement the job search. More support activities include: studying and reading, selecting and preparing references, practicing articulation of *self description* (step one, *Goal setting*), preparing answers to questions likely posed by employers, and writing a daily plan.

A collection of names of contacts, companies, and various other organizations, i.e. trade associations or societies of professionals; along with selected information about each, consti-

Units of Measure

Key Terms Used to Measure Progress During the Job Search

LEAD

Name of employer who can hire now

Wal-Mart Stores, Inc.

CONTACT

Person who provides names • Info

Joe Smith • Aunt Betty

PRIMARY ACTIVITY

Action that secures interviews • Offers

Making a phone presentation
Writing • Mailing a letter
Going on an interview

SUPPORT ACTIVITY

Action that maintains forward thrust of job search

Making trips for supplies
Conducting research
Writing a daily plan

NETWORK

Collection of notes About contacts • Companies Associations

Highlights names • Selected info for each
Electronic file • Handwritten

tutes a **network**. Assemble it by saving as an electronic file and/or handwriting notes. To keep a *network* organized requires tools for filing and retrieving information. (Part two, Companion; *Records Project*.)

Start a Network File

Here are two ways to establish a *network file*. Personal-information-manager software such as XYZ Index, Info Select, Daily Schedule/Calendar, and Access can provide a state-of-the-art information access system. Use it to store, organize, and retrieve information about contacts, companies, and various other organizations. Such applications may also feature an electronic calendar, appointment book, and sections for note making.

If the computer or smart phone is your method of choice, back up all electronic files with hard copy. Or, perhaps you need a low-cost method without a learning curve to assemble your *network*. The traditional, old-fashioned route; a manual system accomplishes the same result.

For a manual system (simple, reliable, mobile, and inexpensive): buy an index-card file, index cards, and separator tabs. Divide the file into two sections, with tabs for A-Z, and 1-31. Place the numbered tabs (each number represents a date of the month) in the front of the file. The alphabet tabs (A-Z), in the back. Either or both ways, keep in touch with contacts and your **network file** remains a helpful tool throughout your career.

> *Network-Filing System*
> **Storage • Retrieval tool**
> Information-manager software
> XYZ Index • Info Select • Etc.
> **File box • Index cards • Dividers**
> Mark tabs 1-31 • A-Z
> Numbered tabs in front
> Lettered tabs in back

• Keep a Profile for each Network Member

The search unfolds as job seekers discover names and assess people (*contacts*) and companies (*leads*). Enter each new name into an electronic file and/or write on an index card. Each entry or card becomes a 'profile in progress' for one member, or, one 'page' in the network.

A **member profile** is a record containing *basic information*; data which partially identifies a person or company (step three, *Prospecting*; Assemble a Network), *summaries of ongoing interaction* with one individual or with employees of one company, and *instructions* for follow through. Get *basic information* from conversations and exchanges, the internet, television, radio, and printed sources. Enter and/or notate the current *phone number(s)* and *addresses* (street, web, and email), so you may phone, text, and write members of your *network*. Record the *job title* of each contact to recognize her/his position in the workplace. Also, add the *type of business* (products/services) of the contact or company.

- **Member-Profile Template**

front

Contact (or) Company Name	Interest Level	Phone Number
Street Address		Web Address
City, State, Zip		
(KEY PERSON)- NAME/TITLE/EXTENSION/EMAIL ADDRESS		
Other Names/Titles/E-Mail Addresses		
Products/Services		

back

Date, Source of Name
Summary of Conversation
Description of correspondence
Instructions for follow-up

If a *member profile* begins with the name of a company, include the *name(s)* and, if accessible, the *e-address* of key employees. Enter and/or write the company's *web address*. Assign a *number* designating the level of your interest to become employed with this company, "1" (very interested), "2" (somewhat interested), and "3" (minimally interested). This rating enables you to compare one company to another and determine the amount of effort you may devote to discovery.

Include the *date* each time you make an entry. This keeps your record current. Note the *source*, from whom or where you got the name of the contact or company. This may be an individual; i.e. *referred by Uncle Jim*, a website or digital listing, a show or ad on television or radio, and an ad, article, or story in a printed medium. This enables you to inform contacts and others unfamiliar with you, how you got their name. Summarize each conversation, exchange, or attempt to interact. Describe simply, any *correspondence*. For example: 'Sent email to thank Jim for....' Also, include *instructions* for following up; action planned for a future date. (Step three, *Prospecting*; Mary Emerson's Member-Profile Format. Step seven, *Closing*; Mary Summarizes Follow-up Activities.)

• Filing Member Profiles

As job seekers communicate with others about their search, two types of people emerge: Those who share knowledge freely and, those reluctant to cooperate. An **active contact** is an individual willing to provide names and useful information helping job seekers advance their progress; and with whom job seekers plan to speak, text, or write about their job search within thirty days. Someone hesitant at first who may help job seekers after a period of thirty days -- is a **contact in reserve.**

If you've an electronic network file, it may automatically arrange profiles alphabetically by the member's name. Enter in your calendar the name and date you plan to communicate with a contact or company. If you use a manual-filing system; for *active contacts*, place each card behind the appropriate (date) numbered tab in the front of the index file. For *contacts in reserve*, place cards behind the alphabet tabs in the rear section by the name of the contact or company. This way, as you retrieve these, you can find them in alphabetical order.

*Arrange Member Profiles
By Name/Date*

Records of contacts • Companies

ELECTRONIC FILE
Sorts profiles automatically

MANUAL FILE
Sort 'active contacts' by date
'Contacts in reserve' alphabetically

Make Ready for Employer Data

In your quest to meet reputable employers, it becomes essential that you know many pertinent details (some of which employers strive to keep hidden from the public) about each employer whom may grant you an interview. For example; age, founder(s), size, ownership, customers, clients, competitors, problems, needs, reputation, types of employees, strengths, weaknesses, exact names of the company and principal employees, the persona of the key employee (person whom would be your supervisor or manager), and the department in which you'd work if hired. In effect, this knowledge distinguishes or 'characterizes' employers. Thus, *essential information* helps job seekers recognize whether an employer is indeed a viable *lead*. (Step three, *Prospecting*; Routing into Industry.)

For each employer in whom you are interested and who may grant you an interview, begin a **prospective-employer profile**. As data is compiled, this becomes a record comprising details helping job seekers expose and, thus, gain greater insight into a company and its employees. (Step three, *Prospecting*; Mary's Prospective-Employer Profile. Part two, Companion; *Records Project*.)

The internet, various publications, contacts, your network file, and interviews are sources for information about prospective employers. As you glean from these more about each *lead*, add notes to the *prospective-employer profile*. Set up an electronic file in a personal-information manager and/or get a letter-size file folder. Name or label these 'Prospective Employers' or 'Leads.' If you've a 'hard' file, arrange employer profiles alphabetically by company name to make them easy to locate and retrieve.

> *Prospective-Employer Profile*
> **Record of Details for One Employer**
> **Stores Basic and Essential Information About:**
> Company • Key Employee(s)
> **Get Data from:**
> Contacts • Employer's website
> Publications • Interviews • Network
> **Prospective-employer profile helps:**
> Characterize employers
> Prepare to interact

Keep Records of Activities

To arrange activities in an orderly and productive fashion, and make it possible to evaluate progress, utilize a *daily schedule*, *chat* and *correspondence logs*. If you prefer, use the computer. A program such as 'Outlook' may serve to organize electronic folders and store information.

Again, taking the traditional route and using a manual system can accomplish the same results at a reduced price: Hard copies of logs and daily schedules

*Evaluate Progress via
Note Making*
To record and arrange activities, keep:
Daily Schedule • Logs
(Chat • Correspondence • Expenses)

may be stored in letter-size, manila, file folders or a three-ring binder. Also, prepare several file folders to sort and store hard copies of letters, resumes, inventories, evaluations, scripts, and other relevant papers such as directions and reference materials.

A **daily schedule** is a list of planned activities and times to perform them each day. It should highlight both *primary* and *support activities*. For example: 'make phone calls from 10 to 11:30 a.m.', 'log on and study ABC Co. and VYZ Construction websites at 11:35 a.m.', 'break from 12:30 to 1:15 p.m.', 'visit with John at the library at 1:30 p.m.', and 'interview with Bill Dallas, Antercom, Inc.at 3:30 p.m.' (Step four, *Planning*; Mary's Daily Schedule.)

The **chat log** is a planner, checklist, and record of telephone conversations or exchanges all in one. It serves three purposes. As a planner, enter the number (goals) of intended or 'projected' presentations (there are four types). As a journal, list the people (contacts) with whom you intend to converse. Note also title, company, phone number, e-address, and who referred them. After you've dialogued, place a checkmark on the log to indicate that you've completed the planned conversations or exchanges. It then becomes a record of activities. Such record may serve to help assess progress and determine where to make adjustments, if necessary. (Step four, *Planning*; Mary's Chat Log and step seven, *Closing*; Mary Logs Completed Calls.)

Maintain a record of each letter, note, email, telegram, etc., in a **correspondence log**. Include the names of contacts and companies (to whom and which company you send correspondence), the purpose (why you send correspondence), and the date. Use the log to trace and confirm communication you send 'snail mail' or electronically to contacts and employers. (Step seven, *Closing*; Mary Emerson's Correspondence Log.)

Job seekers commonly purchase various items and services to implement the search such as books; i.e. *Sure Hire Made Easy*, computer applications, paper, envelopes, stamps, printer, copies, phone and internet service, gasoline, parking fees, etc. Tabulate the cost of such items with an **expenses log**. It serves as a record for tax purposes. Consult a tax advisor to determine which expenditures may be tax deductible. (Part two, Companion; *Records Project*.)

SUMMARY

Organizing is step two of the SDJS. Set in place tools to record and manage, in a precise manner, job-search information and activities. When organized, job seekers make productive use of time and increase efficiency at gathering information. Accurate record keeping enables job seekers to measure progress and recognize where adjustments are needed during the search.

At the start of this section, I define key terms used to measure progress during the SDJS: *lead, contact, primary* and *support activities, network, member profile, active contact,* and *contact in reserve*. A *lead* is the name of a company which represents a legitimate opportunity for job seekers to obtain a respectable job, thus, become meaningfully employed.

A *network* is a collection of *names* of contacts (individuals with whom job seekers interact to advance their job search), companies (leads/prospective employers), various associations of professionals, and *basic information* about each. Obtain a suitable computer application; and/or a file box and index cards with separator tabs, to construct, maintain, and utilize a *network file*. In a manual system, index cards become records or 'profiles.' Each represents a company, association, or individual member of the network. File *member profiles* for *active contacts* numerically, by date. Profiles for *contacts in reserve*, file alphabetically.

Label a file folder 'Prospective Employers' or 'Leads.' This may be electronic and/or letter-size. Use to store forms/pages such as *prospective-employer profiles*. Upon these pages record pertinent details, or '*essential information*,' about leads, so you may characterize them.

A successful job search demands two kinds of activities. *Prima-*

ry activities: efforts undertaken to get interviews and secure job offers. Speaking and corresponding with contacts and employers are primary activities. *Support activities* supplement primary activities. Making trips to get supplies, studying, reading, note making, preparing references, practicing spoken messages which impart details to others, filing information, and writing a daily plan are examples of support activities.

Prepare a *daily schedule* to plan activities (primary and support) and to follow when performing them. Set up a *chat log* to plan and track telephone conversations and online exchanges with contacts and employers. Also, set up *logs* to chronicle *correspondence* and search-related *expenditures*. These tools may be set up electronically via personal-information-management software and/or simply with paper templates. Put in place, several letter-sized file folders to store various papers such as hard copies of letters and resumes, etc. With these tools assembled and ready for use, step two; *Organizing*, is complete. The road ahead is clear. Proceed with step three, *Prospecting*.

3. PROSPECTING
FINDING EMPLOYERS

In this chapter...

Locate your next employer:

- *Read about employers to identify attainable opportunities.*

- *Initiate conversations to discover reputable employers. Those most fit to engage in serious dialogue about hiring you now.*

In this segment, examine how reading, friends, acquaintances, and people in your career field can help identify and shed light on employers who may hire you. Job seekers must first learn about employers if they expect to get a foot in the door.

The more job seekers know about prospective employers, the more ably they may recognize *leads*; those employers interested to discuss employment and offer a legitimate position. Job seekers reach step three of Gopp, Inc.™ *Prospecting*, as they begin gathering information to identify leads. Two productive ways of prospecting under their control are *"reading"* and *"networking."*

> *Prospecting*
> **Process of Gathering Information to Identify Leads**
> **Ways job seekers may control effectively:**
> **READING**
> Utilize printed • Electronic sources for basic facts
> **NETWORKING**
> People become sources for details

Networking is a primary activity where people become sources for minutiae. Here, information is gathered via conversations. Our discussion of networking follows after we explore the merits of reading.

ASSEMBLE A NETWORK

Back in the *Introduction*, I highlight a few questions employers often pose to job seekers. Here's another that presents an opportunity to score points with the employer: *What do you know about our company?* When job seekers provide an answer which conveys clearly they've done their 'homework,' employers are often pleased. So, you ask; How do I construct an answer that wins over the employer?

Locate printed and electronic sources of business information. Read about companies and individuals to determine their suitability as employers. Begin collecting **basic information**: data which partially identifies people and companies such as names, titles, addresses (including web address), phone numbers, nature of business i.e. types of products or services, sales revenues, number of employees, financial analyses, and abbreviated job descriptions. Let's look at the role reading plays in a SDJS. Start at home.

Information at Home

The following sources of business information may be utilized in both their traditional, 'hard' format (if still available in print) and in digital form on the world-wide web. When functioning, the internet offers a highly-efficient method for obtaining information. If you've access, log on.

Community phone books or directories (yellow pages) list companies by products and services. Here are names, phone numbers, addresses, and product advertisements. Often listed, too, are groups of professionals known as industry or trade associations.

Local newspapers (the help-wanted and classified sections), TV and radio stations advertise companies and opportunities regularly. Some even publicize partial job descriptions. Online are numerous "job databases," such as monster.com, jobs.com, indeed.com, and others, which also list company names, contact information, job titles, and bare-bone job descriptions.

Basic Information at Home

TV • Radio • Internet partially identify people & companies:

Names • Addresses • Phone numbers • Products
Job databases • Abridged job descriptions

Local-area phone books:

Products & Services • Names of businesses
Industry & Trade assns • Phone numbers • Ads

Local newspapers • Articles • Ads:

Company names • Addresses • Partial job descriptions

From Community Resources

Within the community, many sources of business information are available. Various organizations accumulate, and may share details about their members.

Call, write, visit in person or online; the Chamber(s) of Commerce and other professional societies, or trade associations in your city or county.

Attend trade shows and fairs. While there, collect company brochures and literature. Seek information about new products and the latest developments in your industry or career field.

Many states and counties fund and operate departments or bureaus which provide public-employment services. Here, public employees and contractors compile lists of jobs and related information about regional businesses. In Maryland, the Maryland Job Service, for instance, is operated by the "Department of Business & Economic Development," MDBED. Check out the website at http://www.choosemaryland.org/. Under business services, click on workforce development.

Visit local businesses, volunteer your services, or, if available, take on a temporary assignment. This places you in direct contact with employers. While there, get a current copy of the company newsletter and other helpful literature.

Credit bureaus and business-reporting agencies collect information about employers. The Better Business Bureau can furnish credit and complaint reports. These may be helpful when job seekers engage with employers in serious discussion about employment. (Step six; *Negotiating*.)

Call, visit a stockbroker's office or website. They circulate annu-

---

More Basic Information in the Community

Call • Visit in person • Online:

Professional societies • Trade associations
Trade shows • Fairs
Public-employment services
Local employers • Credit bureaus
Business-reporting agencies
Stockbroker's office • Libraries

al reports, financial accounts, and other publications of companies whose stock is traded and sold.

Job seekers may continue researching employers by visiting the local-community and university libraries. Find the business-reference or career-resources section. Locate the business directories. Here are some popular ones:

• Business Directories & Databases

The Career Guide. Dun's employment-opportunities directory, Dun's Marketing Services, 2006. This Dun & Bradstreet publication provides leads to employment opportunities at more than 10,000 U.S. companies, including contact information, sales data, number of work divisions, officers and titles. Find additional leads through cross references by geographic area, industry and location, etc.[27] (Frequent library shelf location: CAREER REF 331.128)

D&B's North American Million Dollar Database. Provides information on U.S. and Canadian public and private businesses. Data on companies listed are featured among industry information with up to twenty-four individual eight-digit codes, including size criteria (employees and annual sales), type of ownership, principal executives and biographies. Access to the North American database is available on a subscription basis with the company data being updated every thirty days. Single user, multi-user, LAN, and WAN access configurations are available. For more information about this service, call 1.800.234.3867 (U.S. Customers). [28]

Mergent Manuals (formerly Moody's Manuals, first published in 1918), provide history, operations, subsidiaries, properties, officers, and financial information of thousands of public companies listed on the NYSE and AMEX among various sectors of the economy. I.e. industrial, public utilities, banking & finance, and transportation. Through their subscription service, access their database which includes information on International and U.S. companies. (See Mergent online.)[29]

Standard & Poor's Net Advantage (formerly; Standard And Poor's Register) is a comprehensive database of business and investment information, offering on-line access to Standard & Poor's independent research, including data and commentary on stocks, bonds, funds, and industries. Among many business-related items; it lists telephone numbers, key employee names and titles, sales revenues, products, services, and numbers of employees of numerous corporations.[30]

The Thomas Register of American Manufacturers. For over one hundred years, was known as the "big green books" and "Thomas Registry." First published in 1898 as a single volume by Harvey Mark Thomas as Hardware and Kindred Trades, it grew to be known as "the purchasing bible" and "the bible of industry" by industrial professionals across North America and around the world. In its heyday, it was thirty-four volumes in three sections all of which contained information on industrial products, services, specifications, and product information from thousands of manufacturers. Final hard-copy edition was published in 2006. Today, it's a closely-managed database of industrial companies in North America, indexed by product and service categories. At ThomasNet®, find names, physical locations, and websites.[31]

For decades, researchers have classified business establishments in order to study trends in a productive manner, develop realistic statistical analyses, make projections, and forecast outcomes. The SIC (Standard Industrial Classification) system was adopted and used for sixty years up until 1997. It assigned numerical codes to represent groups of companies conducting similar activities and competing for available business and resources. These were described as "industrial groups."

> ### Business Directories at the Library
> **Employer-specific data arranged for easy access:**
> Dun's Career Guide
> Dun's Million Dollar Database
> Mergent Manuals
> Standard and Poor's Net Advantage
> Thomasnet of American Manufacturers

• What is NAICS?

In April of 1997, SIC's replacement, NAICS (North American Industry Classification System) was placed into effect in the U.S.[32] NAICS assigns each *business establishment* to an **industry** (group of similar companies) based upon activities in which it primarily engages and/or according to services it provides. More than eleven-hundred groups of related industries form **sub-sectors**. The economy in total is divided into twenty large sections referred as **sectors**. These are vast arrays of many industries related by business activity. I.e. information, manufacturing, various services,....

These "sectors" of the economy comprise the major classifications of the NAICS system. Each is represented by a two-digit number. Here's an overview of the way NAICS classifies companies.

North American Industry Classification System (NAICS)
Major Sectors:

11	Agriculture • Forestry Fishing • Hunting
21	Mining
22	Utilities
23	Construction
31-33	Manufacturing
42	Wholesale trade
44,45	Retail trade
48, 49	Transportation • Warehousing
51	Information
52	Finance • Insurance
53	Real estate • Rental • Leasing
54	Professional • Scientific Technical services
55	Management of companies Enterprises
56	Admin. • Waste management Remediation svcs
61	Educational services
62	Health care • Social assistance
71	Arts • Entertainment • Recreation
72	Accomodation • Food services
81	Other services
92	Public administration

• NAICS Hierarchy of Companies

The first two digits identify the industry sector. Mary Emerson found advertising; her chosen field, among the sector encompassing many types of professional services: (54) *Professional, Scientific and Technical Services.* This group contains a vast array of companies or establishments organized to provide a full range of services (either through in-house capabilities or subcontracting), including advice, creative services, account management, production of advertising material, media planning, and buying (i.e. placing advertising).

Then, she determined that the next two digits identify sub sectors, *Advertising, Public Relations* (5418), and *Specialized Design Services* (5414). These groups of related industries comprise establishments primarily engaged in planning, designing, and managing the production of visual communication in order to convey specific messages or concepts, clarify complex information, or project visual identities. These services may include the design of printed materials, packaging, advertising, signage systems, and corporate identification (logos). Such firms may employ commercial artists engaged in generating drawings and illustrations requiring technical accuracy or interpretative skills.

The last two digits identify establishments primarily engaged in creating advertising campaigns and placing such advertising in periodicals, newspapers, radio and television, or other media. These industries include: Advertising Agencies (541810), Media Buying Agencies (541830), Graphic Design Services (541430), Direct Mail Advertising (541860), Media Representatives (541840), and Other Specialized Design Services (541490).

Names of companies, along with profiles which contain *basic information* may be listed under NAICS and other codes, and by industry, in various publications and databanks. I.e. see: www.census.gov/eos/www/naics, Dun & Bradstreet - www.dnb.com, Hoovers - www.hoovers.com, InfoUSA Business Information - www.infousa.com, Manta - www.manta.com, Moody's Investors Service - www.moodys.com, Standard & Poor's - www.standardandpoors.com, IBISWorld - www.ibisworld.com.

Listed under Graphic Design services (541430), Mary found companies such as "Eichner Associates, Inc.," a possible *lead.*

> ## Possible Leads Derived from NAICS Codes
>
> ### Industrial sector
> A large array of industries:
> (54) Professional • Scientific • Technical services
>
> ### Sub sector
> Clusters of related industries:
> (5418) Advertising • Public relations
> (5414) Specialized design services
>
> ### Industry
> A group of similar companies:
> (541430) Graphic design services
>
> ### Company (a possible lead)
> Eichner Associates, Inc.

• In Other Publications

Job Finder books contain *basic information* about companies and services in the private, public, and non-profit sectors. For instance, "Best Jobs for the 21st Century," "150 Best Jobs for a Better World!" are among others which list jobs and descriptions. Shelf location in some libraries is section 650.14.

Newspapers present data about hiring trends, job opportunities, and employers. A review of sections such as the classifieds and help-wanted ads, over the course of three to four months, may reveal employers who advertise repeatedly. This is a reliable indicator of those companies with a high rate of employee turnover.

Professional and trade journals offer insights into current industry events. Often they highlight companies, products, services, and prominent employees. For instance: *PCI, Paint & Coatings Industry* is published monthly by BNP Media of Troy, Michigan. It features news, meetings, shows, education programs, conferences, companies, products; and notes accomplishments of individuals employed in the industry. Like many trade journals, it even contains classified ads which publicize available positions.

> ## More Resources at the Library
> ### Sources for Names • Businesses
> ### Opportunities • Events:
> Job-finder books
> Recent newspapers
> Professional • Trade journals
> Regional phone directories

Regional phone books or directories (the yellow or blue pages) list companies by products and services. Here, you may find phone numbers and addresses of companies located nearby. Some which, for whatever reason, may be omitted from your local-community phone book.

Mary Emerson's Search for Leads

Mary Emerson began her morning at her dining-room table, gathering names and numbers from the newspaper and business listings of her community phone directory. Listed among the want-ads, she discovered two apparent job openings with local companies: 'Ad Specialists,' and 'Advertisers, Ltd.' In the yellow pages, she took note of Avco Creations and Rotaine Enterprises; two likely advertising firms, and the U.S. Chamber of Commerce. Also, she discovered the Association of Graphic Artists, a professional society; two trade organizations (Computer Graphics Association of America; CGAA, and Maryland Association of Agencies & Advertisers; MAAA) and, Graphic Artists Alliance, an association of employers. With her *network file* at the ready, she wrote each name with a corresponding phone number on a blank index card, thus, creating in her network, a *member profile* for each company, firm, society, organization, and association.

Early that afternoon, Mary turned on her computer, logged on-line and 'bookmarked' the web addresses of companies and associations she found in the newspaper and phone book. She linked to the website of the U.S. Chamber of Commerce and studied it. Then, she visited in person, the branch located closest to her town.

The next day, Mary attended a trade show, stopped by her stockbroker's office, and visited two local employers. While driving in the neighborhood and glancing at various offices, she acquired names

> ### *Mary Begins Her Prospecting*
> **At home:**
> Current newspaper • Phone directory
> Online
> **Visits in the community:**
> Chamber of commerce • Trade fairs
> Stockbroker's office • Local employers
> **At the library:**
> Business directories • Databases • Trade journals
> Recent newspapers • Regional phone directories
> Computer files

of prospective employers. That evening, she logged on and examined the websites she noted the day before.

The following day, she visited the library to investigate local employers and hiring trends in the advertising field. There, she checked business directories, trade journals, recent newspapers, regional phone directories, and even logged on to the library's computer.

Mary carried blank index cards with her when she traveled away from home, so she could notate on the spot *basic information* about individuals and businesses. Taking advantage of the available resources in her community, she identified employers and others about whom she wanted to know more. She wrote each of these names on the front of a separate index card. On the back, she noted the date and source from where she got the name. Then, she placed these in the front of her (manual) *network file*.

Yellow pages
AGA • Avco Creations
CGAA • GAA • MAAA
Rotaine Enterprises
U.S. Chamber of Commerce

Newspapers
Ad Specialists
Advertisers, Ltd.

Chamber of commerce
Finch Advertising
Golson Advertising

Trade show
Express Printing
Publican Industries, Inc.

**Business directories
(NAICS code 541430)**
Eichner Associates, Inc.
Erlitch-Maines, Inc.
Image Dynastics, Inc.
Kenerday Associates
(NAICS code 541810)
Garnett Company, Inc.

Visible in the neighborhood
Smith Barney • FedEx Office

• Mary Launches a Network

At the end of each day, Mary entered the notes on her index cards into her computer. Thus, she created an electronic *member profile* for each company, organization, or individual. As she added new profiles and more information to each, she grew her (electronic) network.

The internet represents a virtual treasure trove of current information about prospective employers. With leads selected (like Mary's sample above), begin a *member profile* for each. Visit their websites by logging on. Here, find and note address(es), phone(s), information about employees, history, products, services, and more. Keep in mind, however, what employers reveal online about themselves is edited closely for public scrutiny. Employers expect job seekers to know this *basic information*. Therefore, you must learn more to keep ahead of the pack! Next, we discuss how *networking* propels you toward, and then, ultimately into the job market.

- **Mary's Initial Member Profiles Via Reading**

Smith Barney
Rotaine Enterprises
Publican Industries, Inc.
Md Assn Ag & Adv-
Kenerday Associates
Image Dynastics, Inc.
Graphic Artists Alliance
Golson Advertising
Garnett Company, Inc.
Finch Advertising
FedEx Office
Express Printing
Erlitch-Maines, Inc.
Eichner Associates, Inc.
Comp Grph Assn Am
Chamber of Commerce
Avco Creations
Assn of Graphic Artists
Advertisers, Ltd.
Ad Specialists

CHARACTERIZE EMPLOYERS VIA CONVERSATIONS

The more knowledge, about leads, job seekers accumulate -- the more those leads become viable. The more realistic the leads, the more confident are job seekers about approaching employers for interviews. A way to collect data essential for determining if leads are viable is through "networking."

Networking refers to gathering information about employers and others from conversations. When asked, people (*contacts*) often provide names and information about themselves, other people, and prospective employers. To make a network functional, job seekers need grow the number of *contacts* (expanding the network) and gather details about employers. Begin networking by asking someone you know to share the names of people s/he knows. Then, ask those people to refer others they know, and so on. In theory, networking produces a chain of over a thousand names at the tenth level.[33] A name of an individual or company given the job seeker by a contact during a conversation becomes a *referral*.

Effective Networking Produces Referrals

Think of relatives, friends, and acquaintances, those who may be willing to provide *referrals* and information, facilitating your

Begin with Individuals You Know!

Relatives • Friends (close • distant)
Friends of family members
Neighbors • Church members • Clergy
Dentist • Doctor • Realtor • Lawyer • Accountant
Neighborhood-bank tellers • Manager
Stockbroker • Insurance agent • Librarian
Grocer • Butcher • Jeweler • Hair dresser • Barber
Property manager • Maintenance persons • Landlord
Mail person • Painter • Carpenter • Landscaper
Interior designer • Mechanic • Former teachers
Fellow alumni • Members of clubs • Teams

progress. Start with twenty to twenty-five names. Write each name on a separate index card. And, or, begin a page in an electronic file.

• The Network Presentation

With a filing system in place (step two, *Organizing*), prepare to talk with contacts. Remember, though networking should proceed in a relaxed and friendly fashion, its purpose is greater than mere "socializing."

Polish with Repetition
Your Network Presentation
Job seeker initiates dialogue w/ contacts:
Relatives • Friends • Acquaintances • Referrals
Scripted in 4 steps:
Attention-Grabber • Identify • Payoff • Signoff

The **network presentation** is a conversation initiated by the job seeker with a relative, friend, acquaintance, or referral. This may occur face-to-face, on the telephone, or online. Opportunities to dialogue online abound. Sites such as www.jibberjobber.com/, www.linkedin.com/, www.twitter.com/, www.jobangel.com/, and others may prove fruitful. However, if you choose to utilize the internet for networking, be selective. It's easy to get distracted by limitless possibilities and individuals unknown to you. Keep all conversations focused on gathering relevant information you need to advance and conclude your job search. Prepare for conversations by scripting your part. Follow the *four-step formula: Attention-Grabber, Identify, Payoff,* and *Signoff.* This keeps you in control. (Part two, Companion; *Network-Presentation Guide*).

During an exercise class at her health spa, Mary Emerson became acquainted with Dick Metcalf; a retired attorney. Shortly thereafter, when she was alone and could comfortably write, she noted his name, street, and city, thus starting a *member profile* for Dick. Two days later, she called on the phone to chat with him. Flattered by Mary's request, Dick was receptive to the idea of providing his advice and perhaps sharing some personal knowledge. Here's Mary's network-presentation script (note the *four-step formula*).

• Mary's Network-Presentation Script

Attention-Grabber

Hello Dick, this is Mary Emerson. Perhaps you recall chatting briefly during our aerobics class, Tuesday evening at the health spa. I trust you enjoyed the workout. Feeling well, today?

Dick, I am prospecting in search of my next employer: One with a fine reputation and the wherewithal to offer me a meaningful position. I'd like to have your advice.

Can you chat a few minutes?

Identify

Dick, let me refresh your memory on my background. I've been in the advertising field for three years researching, creating, and composing various print and video projects. I write, edit, design and produce camera-ready artwork on the computer. I have a BA in Communication Arts and received the Goucher Award for creative graphics. I'm a member of the American Marketing Association. I've organized discussions among colleagues to learn more about the advertising industry.

I have a few questions for you. Okay?

Payoff

Who do you know works in the advertising field?

Where does she work? What's her job title? Do you know who works with her? Has she ever mentioned any of her problems at work? What's her phone number?

Who do you know may know someone in advertising?

Who do you know who's well-known and widely respected?

What does he do? How do you know him? How do I reach him?

Signoff

Thanks for your time and suggestions, Dick. Let me know when I may help you. My number is (301) 555-0100. Email is mtemerson@xyzmail.com.

May I mention to others that we spoke? I'd like to keep you informed of my progress. Okay? Do I have your name and address correct? Any other numbers where I can call you? May I send an e-mail? What's your e-mail address?

I welcome any ideas, thoughts, or information you hear that may be relevant. Thanks again.

Dick referred to Mary the names of two people. A momentary lapse, he couldn't recall where one, Bob Gerber, is employed. He did recall, however, that Kitty Weldon works at Mehcom, Inc. Mary created a *member profile* for each *referral*. She then added these to the date (1-31) section of her *network file*. The illustration below is for Kitty Weldon.

• Mary Emerson's Member-Profile Format

front

Mehcom, Inc.	2	301-555-0125
2930 Suiznet Road #5 Avon Heights, MD 20787		www.mehcom.com

Bill Jonas-Sales manager -ext.659

Kitty Weldon-Sec.

Sell print advertising services

back

> *3/25-Dick Metcalf is a friend of Kitty Weldon.*
>
> *3/26-Spoke with Kitty. Told me about Jonas.*
>
> *email: kweldon@mehcom.com. Sent email to thank Kitty. Try back tomorrow at 1:30.*

• Routing into Industry

Networking takes job seekers directly into the job market when they talk with contacts who work in their (prospective) career field. An **industry contact** is someone associated with a career field or industry able to provide industry-specific information about people and companies.

This person may be a client, employee, supplier, commercial banker, contractor, or competitor of any of your leads. You may or may not know her or him. In fact, prospective and former employers, co-workers, and colleagues may be industry contacts, too.

Generally, industry contacts are knowledgeable about their career field including current trends and developments. They represent 'shortcuts' to interviews and job offers because they can reveal **essential information**; pertinent details enabling job seekers to characterize employers, such as: company personality, characteristics of model employees, present projects and plans, key customers, main competitors; employer problems, needs, negatives, and concerns; flaws related to image and reputation, complaints, company/employee strengths and weaknesses.

A planned conversation initiated by the job seeker with an industry contact, becomes an **industry-contact presentation**. To prepare for such a dialogue, before placing the phone call, visit the website of the company that employs the industry contact. Familiarize yourself with the basic facts about the industry-contact's company (employer). Create a *member profile* and, then, script your part. Again, follow the *four-step formula*. This keeps you in control. (Part two, Companion; *Industry-Contact-Presentation Guide*).

> ### *Industry-Contact Presentation*
> **Job seeker initiates dialogue w/ person able to provide industry-specific info, industry contact works (has worked) in job seeker's career field • Or allied industry:**
> Employer • Employee • Former colleague
> Commercial banker • Supplier • Contractor
> **Scripted in 4 steps:**
> Attention-Grabber • Identify • Payoff • Signoff

• Networking Industry Contacts Effectively

Let's return to our fictional, self-directed job seeker, Mary Emerson. One of the questions Mary asks each *contact* with whom she chats; "Who do you know works in the advertising field?" (Mary's Network-Presentation Script, *Payoff*, p.52). Simply asking this question to her relatives, friends and acquaintances; Mary learns names of people who work in her chosen field.

Having knowledge of their names and phone numbers, Mary may now reach out and chat with *industry contacts*. As she engages them she may learn *essential information* about employers in her field. Some may even request to meet with her.

A face-to-face meeting during the prospecting step of the job search is sometimes called a **research** or **information interview**. If invited, meet face-to-face when, as a result, a job interview with a reputable employer seems highly likely and a job offer is a possible outcome. Until you're certain the invitation is genuine, however, choose a neutral location in a public place. Otherwise, talk with *industry contacts* by phone. If an online exchange is the preferred choice of the *industry contact*, this medium may also prove productive.

Before phoning Jim Everett, an *industry contact*; Mary visited the website of Cobson Industries, Jim's employer. There, she familiarized herself with *basic information* about Jim's company. She prepared a *member profile* and a script to guide her conversation. Then, she proceeded with a call to Jim, at his work.

Mary's telephone call to Jim Everett of Cobson Industries illustrates her approach, step by step:

> ### *Be Selective to Meet Industry Contacts*
> **If invited, meet industry contacts in person when advantageous:**
> If interview w/ an employer is likely result
> When job offer is probable
> **Otherwise converse by:**
> Telephone • Online exchange

• Mary's Industry-Contact Presentation Script

Attention-Grabber

Good morning, am I speaking with Jim Everett? Hello, Jim.
This is Mary Emerson. I'm calling from Wheaton.
Don Riggs, with the Chamber of Commerce, whom I believe you know; suggested to call you. I hope this is a convenient time.

Jim, I'm prospecting in search of my next employer. Don felt your advice would be sound and thoughtful. Can you chat for a few minutes?

Identify

Jim, I've been in the advertising field for three years researching, creating, and composing various print and video projects. I write, edit, design and produce camera-ready artwork on the computer. I have a BA in Communication Arts and received the Goucher Award for creative graphics. I'm a member of the American Marketing Association. I've organized discussions among colleagues to learn more about the advertising industry.

I'd appreciate some answers to a few questions. Okay?

Payoff

Which are the top three or four companies in the industry? What openings are you aware of in the industry? Who do you suggest I talk to there? What do you know about her? Does she make hiring decisions?

Are you familiar with Publican Industries? Who do you know works there? Please, tell me more about him. Background? Describe his persona. Notable achievements? What do you know about Avco Creations? What else do you know about Avco? Problems? Negatives? Weaknesses? What's their reputation like? Tell me something about them I wouldn't find on their website? Which companies would you recommend I avoid? Why?

Can you share some information about Cobson? What exactly do you do for Cobson Industries? For how long? What's your background? What do you like most about your job? How's your business been during the past few months?

What's Cobson's present sales volume? Describe a typical client. What are current developments? What problems is your business facing? How do you scout new talent? If there was an opening at Cobson for a sales representative, whom would I call? What's her title? What types of people does she hire? What more can you tell me about her?

Signoff

Jim, I thank you very much for sharing your time and advice. Let me know if I may help you. May I have permission to mention to others that we've spoken?

May I give you my phone number and email? Mary Emerson, 301 555-0100, and mtemerson@xyzmail.com. Have I spelled your name correctly? I wish to keep you informed of my progress. Is that okay? May I call you in the evening at home? What's the number? Mobile phone? Number? When's it best to call? May I send an email? What's your e-address? Street address? I'd welcome additional ideas or thoughts you may have, or anything you hear that might be relevant. Thanks again.

55

Record all Calls

The following technique may help keep conversations with contacts and employers productive. Though it may be enticing to seize opportunities to meet with contacts, the telephone allows for sufficient exposure. It enables job seekers to dialogue quickly, economically, and efficiently.

Therefore, with few exceptions, conduct networking conversations by phone. And, -- record them! (In fact, *record all telephone conversations connected with your job search.*) This saves time, frees you from taking notes while on the phone, and creates an accurate record of conversations. (Request from the other party, if necessary, permission to record. See USCS Title 18, section 2510. In Maryland, see Annotated Code of Maryland, title 10, subtitle 4, section 10-402.)

Recording Phone Calls
Consider these advantages:
Reduces distractions
Provides for accurate record
Allows for critique
Helps improve technique
Equipment needed:
Cassette • Digital recorder
Telephone 'pickup' • Tapes

Generally, networking conversations pay off quickly. You learn names and information about contacts, businesses, organizations, employers, and job opportunities. Begin a *member profile* for each. Notate index cards and place these into your manual *network file*, and/or enter the data into an electronic folder.

Mary grew her network of contacts and companies initiating conversations beginning with individuals she knows (i.e. her uncle; Jim Emerson, and her aunt; Betty Thomas). She added member profiles for each organization, company, and contact referred to her. She filed the cards in the front section of her network file (manual), by the date (1-31) on which she intended to communicate with each contact, company, etc.

• Mary Expands her Network Via Networking

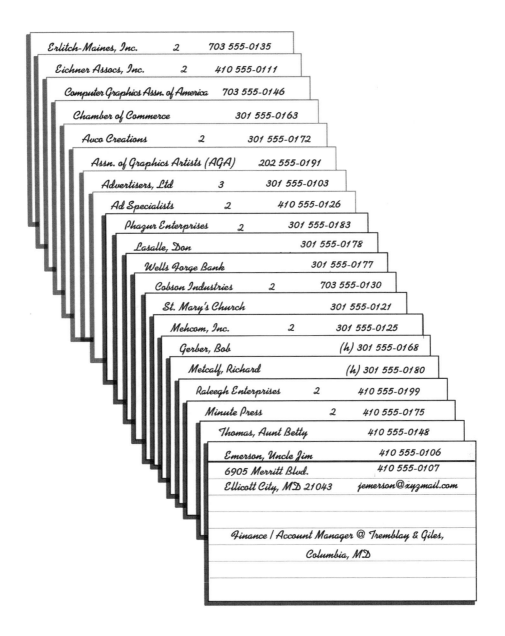

Mary discovered Publican Industries, at their exhibit, while attending a local trade show. Upon learning the nature of their business, she became intrigued. As Mary learned basic facts reading about Publican Industries and pertinent details from networking, she compiled relevant points, thus, building a helpful *prospective-employer profile*. (Part two, Companion; *Records Project*).

• Mary's Prospective-Employer Profile

Employer

Name: *Publican Industries, Inc.*

Address: *1032 Whitesford Place*

City: *Silver Spring* State *Maryland* Zip *20910*

Phone number: *301-555-0147*

Web address: *www.publicanind.com*

Receptionist name(s): *Angie Blackwell*

Key Employee

Name *Robert Anderson Stiles, Jr.*

Title *VP Sales* Email: *rastiles@publicanind.com*

Extension # *67* Mobile: *301-555-0152* Home: *703-555-0134*

Related information: *6 years with Publican. Manages sales dept. Reports to co. president, Ed Knoll. 15 years in advertising. Married. 3 kids. Fan of "Redskins." Golfer. Eats at "Alfredos."*

Secretary name: *Susan Darnell* **Email:** *susand@publicanind.com*

Related information: *1 year w/Publican. Lives in Silver Spring.*

Department Description

Size *3 Sales employees* Position Titles *Adv. Rep.*

Job Description *Sell advertising services in local territory*

Employee profile / Background *Creative, persuasive, friendly, organized. College educated 2-3 years of sales experience.*

Names/Titles: *John Turley, Jill Brown, Bill Asher (all reps)*

Company Information

Founded:	*1969*
Founder(s):	*Don Publick, John Candle*
Products/ Services:	*Full line print, video advertising services*
Employees:	*60*
Revenues	*$8 million*

Market share:	*4.5%*
Type of ownership:	*Private*
Parent company:	*n/a*
Affiliates:	*n/a*
Subsidiaries:	*Owin Printing*
Geographic activity:	*Mid-Atlantic states*
Typical clients:	*Banks, OEM's trade assns., non-profit orgs.*
Main competitors:	*Golson Advertising, Emerson Promotions*
Company personality:	*Team, service & growth oriented, aggressive*
Current developments:	*Looking to update computer system for account admin. On target to exceed last year's sales by twelve percent.*
Company goals:	*25% more video projects. Increase market share to 5%.*
Current problems/Needs:	*Data entry. Looking to improve present method of processing account information.*
Hiring procedure:	*2 interviews: 1st w/VP, 2nd w/Pres.*
Model employee profile:	*2-3 years in advertising business, team player*
Employee turnover:	*Low, except sales dept. (avg. length 15 mos.)*
Industry reputation:	*Excellent (per references)*
References:	*Jack Hill-CFR Bank; Dick Green-Video Notions*
Credit/ Complaints:	*Excellent/few insignificant (per BBB, TRW, Dan Bow--TJ Supply, company website)*
Literature:	*Obtained company brochure at trade show.*
Notable points:	*Recognized by CGA, MAAA. Stable & flexible. Website is helpful, easy-to-use, and carefully designed.*
Directions to office:	*95N Exit 5(N). 2 lights (L) on Whitesford.*

SUMMARY

Prospecting, step three of the SDJS, is the process of gathering information to identify potential job opportunities (*leads*). Job seekers learn, by *reading* and *networking*, which prospective employers are most suited and able to offer a meaningful opportunity. The more leads, and the more job seekers know about those leads; the greater their level of confidence for pursuing interviews.

Begin assembling a '*network*;' a collection of names and information about contacts, companies, associations, and organizations. Employment-related information is readily available in print. Read newspapers, job-finder books and magazines, phone and business directories, trade journals, business newsletters and reports, community bulletin boards, etc.

More employment information streams over the airwaves and sound systems from television, radio, and various community events.

Ever more data, easily-accessible online; is stored electronically in computer files, websites, electronic databases, and shared through networks.

For each contact, company, and organization about which you desire to learn more, gather information from printed, broadcast, and electronic sources. Write on an index card and/or enter into a computer record, *basic information*: names, titles, addresses, phone numbers, types of products or services, and abbreviated job descriptions. Each becomes a *member profile* in progress. Store member profiles in an index-card file (manual) and/or utilize an electronic folder (digital).

Next, tap into another huge source of information: people. Grow your network by means of *networking*; the process of gathering information from conversations. Gain access to others' personal knowledge, through the spoken word. Call on the telephone individuals who may dialogue with you. From them, learn names (*referrals*) and get details about employers.

Frame carefully, your request for information. Prepare scripts to guide conversations. When making phone presentations, follow scripts. Use the *four-step formula*: *Attention-Grabber, Identify, Payoff, Signoff*. This keeps you in control.

Initiate conversations beginning with relatives, friends, and acquaintances. Always be courteous. Remain acutely aware of each contact's willingness to provide information and referrals. Strive to obtain two or more new names, from each *network presentation*. Leave with contacts; your name, phone number, and e-mail address (if applicable). Record phone calls digitally, or on audio tape. When undistracted, review recordings and write relevant information onto index cards and place these in your *network file*. And/or enter into an electronic version.

To determine which employers represent viable *leads*, talk with *industry contacts*. These are individuals associated with an industry (former and current employees, clients, suppliers, commercial bankers, contractors, and competitors of your leads). They can provide *essential information*: pertinent details enabling job seekers to characterize employers. Prior to making *industry-contact presentations*, examine the website of the company that employs the industry contact, begin a member profile, and, then, prepare a script.

Endeavor to identify one or more viable leads each day. Compile facts about each company or individual you believe has a job opening, or; the foresight and wherewithal to generate a suitable opportunity. Begin and continue filling in a *prospective-employer profile*. Store these in a 'hard' and/or 'electronic' file: 'Prospective Employers,' or 'Leads.' Primed with *basic* and *essential information*, job seekers enable themselves to identify and characterize leads. To find those reputable employers, most fit to gain, who will open their doors and talk seriously about legitimate job prospects.

Next, we'll see how planning, or lack of it, can make or break a job search.

4. PLANNING

PREPARING TO INTERACT WITH EMPLOYERS

IN THIS CHAPTER...

Arrange to meet employers:

- *Identify, list, and prove your skills.*
- *Fashion a script to help make dynamic phone calls. Get employers to pick up the telephone when you call. Convey, with confidence, your message.*
- *Chart a course for your progress.*

Although planning has become a staple of business vernacular, it's often overlooked. To proceed without it, job seekers rely upon hope; that their words and actions bring them good fortune, chance; that they arrive in the right place at the right time, and trust; that others will act swiftly. This is, at best, a scattered approach to running a job search. Conversely, job seekers who desire a short and successful search must rely less upon luck, minimize risk, and place their faith in self. This may be accomplished simply by assuming control over the search. Careful planning yields a reliable formula for obtaining job interviews and subsequent offers of employment.

In step four, **_Planning_** (the second P of the Gopp, Inc.™ plan), the job seeker prepares a self presentation, arranges to meet employers, and manages closely her/his time. In the first stage, we cover the "skills presentation." Next, we dissect the employer-telephone presentation

> ### *Planning*
> **Formula to Interact With Employers**
> #### SKILLS PRESENTATION
> A "verbal portrait"
> Portrays skills/ Accomplishments
> Stresses benefits to employer
> Supported by examples
> #### SCRIPT FOR TELEPHONE CONVERSATION
> Depict potential value
> Satisfy employer needs
> To secure meetings w/ employers
> Via phone calls
> #### SCHEDULE FOR DAILY ACTIVITIES
> To arrange time efficiently

in all its pieces. We conclude with suggestions for scheduling daily activities to manage time efficiently. All under the control of the job seeker!

GIVE 'EM A SKILL SET THEY CAN'T RESIST

Studies indicate that over eighty percent of job seekers are unable to clearly articulate their skills to employers.[34] To accurately convey your worth, employers need to know what you can bring to the table as an employee. Convince employers of your talents through a prepared *skills presentation*:

A verbal portrait of a job seeker's achievements and future potential in terms easily understood by employers. This spoken summary should be concise, well-defined, and supported by examples. An effective skills presentation focuses on relevant skills and accomplishments. It emphasizes benefits (gain) the employer can expect, should s/he hire you. Let's begin by focusing on skills.

Skill Categories

Recall from the *personal assessment* (step one, *Goal setting*) that a *skill* is a developed ability, something a person does well. Before you talk to employers, identify skills that best describe your abilities as you perceive them. There are three types: *self-management, transferable*, and *job-related*.

• What are Self-Management Skills?

As part of reputable employers' evaluation of candidates for hire, they assess self-management skills. Think of *self-management skills* as personality traits or strengths. These basic abilities are innate and learned.

> *Begin With What You Do Well*
> **List skills in three areas:**
> Self-management
> Transferable
> Job-related

They're necessary for healthy social adaptation. And, yes, even success at job searching!

Self-management skills become productive-worker qualities when employees combine and cooperate with others on the job. Examples include: *prompt, properly attired* and *groomed, assertive, ambitious*, and *enthusiastic* (Revisit Introduction, How Employers Evaluate Job Seekers?)

> ### To Get Along With Others
> **Self-management skills are basic abilities:**
> Dress • Grooming
> Arriving on time
> Fundamental communication
> Team up w/ co-workers
> Desire to work
> Sense of humor • Honesty

• What Are Transferable Skills?

Advanced-level abilities known as ***transferable skills*** enable employees to perform general tasks. They're required in practically every job. We acquire transferable skills throughout life. Like self-management skills, they're portable from one job to another. Two transferable skills high on the employer's list include: *solve problems* and *communicate ideas clearly*. To *plan, teach, administer, evaluate*, and *lead* are also important transferable skills.

> ### To Perform General Tasks
> **Transferable skills are advanced-level abilities:**
> Speak and Write clearly • Organize
> Manage projects • Solve problems
> Initiate new tasks • Instruct others effectively
> Comprehend assignments • Follow instructions

• What are Job-Related Skills?

The third type, ***job-related skills*** enable employees to perform job-specific tasks: to *operate computers, read blueprints, design software*, etc. We attain these highly-advanced abilities through intensive education and training, and, then, applying them on the job. To remain employed in a shrinking job market, employees must possess or acquire job-related skills.

Employees may be observed exhibiting these skills while performing in four areas of business activities. Three of these; Data, Ideas, and People, require abstract thinking. Examples of abilities, here, in these areas, include: *interpret market studies, prepare financial statements, create advertising slogans, craft news copy, counsel students,* and *chair a board of directors.* The fourth area; Things, requires manual dexterity, i.e. the ability to *draft product schematics,* or *perform a dental prophylaxis.*

> ### To Perform Specific Tasks in Each Area of Business
>
> **Job-related skills are highly-advanced abilities:**
>
> **DATA**
> Interpret market studies
> Prepare financial statements
>
> **IDEAS**
> Create advertising slogans
> Craft news copy
>
> **PEOPLE**
> Counsel students
> Chair board of directors
>
> **THINGS**
> Draft product schematics
> Operate construction equipment

Prove Skills with Examples

Job seekers must convince employers their skills are valuable. To do this, they must first prove they possess desirable skills, and, then, link them to job performance. Let's see how this is done.

To prove you own a skill, provide **examples**: clear, convincing descriptions of past events when something noteworthy was achieved. Use concise language. If, for instance, you say you're able to "organize," support this claim describing how, in the past, you succeeded at organizing something. To prove skills, let's examine another four-step system. We call this, 'Prove It!'

The first step is to *qualify*. Begin your examples with names, dates, and places. Use the five "W's." Explain "who" or "what" the example is about, and "when," "where," and "why" did it happen? Let's trace an example from Mary Emerson's proof:

• The 'Prove It' System

Mary claims she's able to "analyze spreadsheet data" (a job-related skill). As she begins, she *qualifies*:

"Last September, Grayson's MIS manager, John Abbott, was given the task to streamline data-entry procedures in my division. He selected me to coordinate the creation of technical manuals for updating our data-entry people about spreadsheet analysis."

The next step is to *quantify* the skill example. In this step, Mary quantifies the example in numbers and measurable data (inches, dollars, quotas, etc.). She answers the questions: How much? How many? How big?

"The division had six full-time employees working in data entry. I had six weeks to analyze MS Excel spreadsheet data and determine how it could be integrated from Wordperfect files. The job required the creation of two technical manuals."

Next, Mary describes an *activity* associated with the example. She answers the question: What did you do? Then, she explains the *result* produced by her action (an accomplishment):

> **'PROVE IT!'**
> **Four steps to convincing examples:**
> **QUALIFY**
> Names • Dates • Places
> Who • What is it about?
> When • Where
> Why has it happened?
> **QUANTIFY**
> Numbers • Data
> How much? • How many?
> How big?
> **ACTION/RESULT**
> Describe activity
> What happened?
> What resulted?
> **LINK-UP**
> Describe impact on others

"I researched a few existing systems. From these, I devised a modified version to evaluate our employees' skills. Per my evaluation, the company paid $6,000 for training to upgrade the skill levels of three employees assigned to the project. As a result, seventy-five percent more spreadsheet data were processed within a thirty-day test period. Consequently, the decision to have to hire a subcontractor (at an estimated cost of $25,000) was averted."

Finally, Mary *links-up* her skill example. She describes how someone else gained (benefited) because she applied her skill. (Here, her former employer is the beneficiary):

"My ability to analyze spreadsheet data enabled my former employer to increase productivity and contain costs for labor."

To prove your skills, consider nine skill descriptors (three of each type). Begin with *self-management skills*. Select those which reflect your strong points, and connect clearly with the job you seek. (For samples: Part two, Companion, *Skills Project*.) To illustrate the skills identification-and-development process, we'll trace Mary Emerson's choices:

• Mary Emerson's Skills Inventory

Self-Management Skills
Persistent • *Creative*
Resourceful

Transferable Skills
Organize • *Solve problems*
Lead others

Job-Related Skills
Analyze spreadsheet data
Develop • *Service clientele*
Advise industry managers

Next, prepare examples. You may need convey two or three examples to convince employers you possess a skill. Prepare three examples for each skill. Here, Mary prepares a skill example. (For blanks: Part two, Companion, *Skills Project*.)

• Mary's Self-Management Skill Example

Skill Name: *Persistent*

Qualify: *After graduating from the University of Maryland I sought a job with the Grayson Corporation, one of the top advertising firms in the area. I heard their Director of Media Services, Bob Hargrove, was competent and personable.*

Quantify: *Grayson had an opening in media services. At that time, this was a department of six people. Someone had moved and there was a vacancy.*

Action/Result: *I called Bob Hargrove. He told me they were interested in people with more experience. I refused to accept that. I then spoke with three people in the department to learn about the responsibilities of the job and some of the problems they were experiencing at the time. I then called Bob back, and, as a result, got the interview and the job!*

Link-up: *My persistence enabled Bob Hargrove to solve a problem and save money. After I accepted the job, he told me I saved him time and money because the vacancy was filled quickly with little effort.*

• Accomplishments: The Measure of Skills

Accomplishments are linked closely with skills. Actually, skills may be confirmed by accomplishments. An ***accomplishment*** is an event at which a person attains something of value as a result of training, planning, and hard work. Accomplishments are measurable and may be concisely described using short phrases.

People become accomplished in three areas of life: in their professions or jobs (work), in education/training (school), and at home or outside the home (community).

> *Show 'em What You've Done*
> **Accomplishment**
> Event at which value attained • Measurable
> Described concisely
> **Three areas**
> On the job (Work) • Education • Training (School)
> At/Outside home (Community)

To identify accomplishments, refer to the "result" of the action/result section of your skills examples. (Part two, Companion; *Skills Project*)

After generating her skills examples, Mary referred to the "result" of the action/result section to define her accomplishments. She selected nine related to her job search. She then listed these on the *Accomplishments Inventory*.

• Mary Emerson's Accomplishments Inventory

Transfer nine accomplishments from the Action/Result section of your skills examples and edit as needed. List them in order of importance, the most notable first.

1. 5 new projects for Grayson Corporation
2. 75% increase of data entry at Grayson Corporation
3. Met 25 consecutive deadlines
4. Goucher award
5. Job offer with Grayson Corporation
6. Nominated as regional representative for AMA
7. Selected of 5 co-workers to assist division manager
8. BA Communication Arts
9. Paid 75% of college education

We identified three kinds of skills: *self-management*, *transferable*, and *job-related*. We stressed the importance of using *examples* to prove to employers you possess skills. We illustrated a system for assembling examples. Then, we saw how skills may be expressed in concise, economical language, as *accomplishments*.

Now, let's see how accomplishments may be *linked* with benefits employers expect to obtain when hiring someone new.

• Employer Benefits

For employers to compete, and thus, to survive, they need to increase profits, solve problems, make employees efficient, provide effective management, and more. These gains or 'improvements' represent **benefits** to employers. Consequently, employers want to know how job seekers may provide them *benefits*. Remember, employers seldom hire people just because they look good on paper or seem to possess desirable skills or qualities. Therefore, job seekers must convince employers that their accomplishments represent benefits.

Give 'em What They Need
Benefit
Anticipated event • Something job seeker offers employer
Linked to accomplishment
Possible gain for employer's business

• Samples of Benefits

Save time	Satisfy customers	Enhance company's image
Develop new products	Alleviate stress on employees	Free up key employees
Recognize •	Increase productivity	Increase revenues
Solve problems	Establish new business	Train personnel
Reduce accidents	Reduce • Manage waste	
Save money		

Benefits cover a range of activities and solutions. Determine benefits you may provide employers. To each *accomplishment* you describe in the action/result section of your skills examples, and then, list on the accomplishments inventory; link a corresponding *benefit*. (Part two, Companion; *Skills Project*.)

Mary listed nine accomplishments on the *Benefits Inventory* (right column). She then listed a benefit in connection with each accomplishment, in the left column.

• Mary Emerson's Benefits Inventory

Copy your accomplishments below in the right column. Link the benefit an employer may receive in connection with each accomplishment and write it in the left column.

BENEFIT	ACCOMPLISHMENT
1. Create new business	5 new projects for Grayson
2. Increase productivity	75% increase data entry
3. Save time	Met 25 consecutive deadlines
4. Enhance credibility	Goucher award
5. Persuade clients	Job offer/Grayson
6. Reduce pressure on leaders	AMA nomination
7. Free up key employees	Co-managed critical project
8. Complete assignments	BA degree
9. Save money	Paid 75% of education

In *Prospecting*, step three, job seekers identify employers interested in discussing employment and able to offer a legitimate position. The *skills presentation* begins as an exercise, preparing job seekers to persuade employers of their abilities. When job seekers identify viable *leads* (prospective employers), list *skills*, prepare *examples*, chronicle *accomplishments*, and, then, determine *benefits* to offer employers; they're ready to forge an approach. In this next section, follow the road leading to employers and, thus, interviews.

THERE'S AN IMPORTANT CALL FOR YOU, MR. EMPLOYER

Job seekers secure more interviews via the telephone than by any other method.[35] As many as twenty-five percent of polished telephone presentations result in interviews. Often, they produce leads.[36] The phone is convenient and establishes the possibility for immediate results. When they contact employers by phone, job seekers get distraction-free exposure at minimal cost. It provides an opportunity to demonstrate fundamental-communication skills. As job seekers self present repeatedly to employers, they build confidence and improve their presentation.

> *Advantages of Phone to Arrange Interviews:*
>
> **Ample exposure at nominal cost**
> Fast • Convenient • Validates skills
> Improves confidence • Presentation
> 20-25% calls result in interviews

Still, some people remain reluctant to use the phone in this manner. If you feel uncomfortable about approaching virtual strangers (employers unknown to you), keep the following in mind:

Perceptive Employers are Receptive

Job seekers don't impose on employers when they call and politely, yet firmly, request a meeting. Statistics indicate the 'hidden job market' is enormous. Employers must find ways, in addition to advertising and word-of-mouth, to identify competent individuals and hire them. By phoning employers, you actually help make their jobs easier!

> *You Can Simplify Their Job*
> **By phoning employers they may:**
> Learn from you • Consider you for current opening
> Replace a marginal employee • Create a new position •
> Assess your talent • Fulfill company policy • Refer others

Jobs are Offered by Employers

Let's review what we mean by an **employer:** a company, corporation, business, organization—or individual—who hires and compensates workers. With few exceptions, hires require approval from a person, often distinguished by a number of loosely-fitting names such as: *"decision maker," "target person," "hiring agent,"* and *"hiring authority."* All identify the employer. Such a person may be the business owner, president, vice-president; department, division, area or facility manager. Some may include co-workers in their decision. Along the road leading to a suitable job offer, job seekers meet the realization that they must speak with the person who makes or participates in the decision to hire (the prospective boss).

> *The One With the Authority to Hire*
> **Phone leads • Talk w/ employer**
> **Person who makes hiring decision:**
> Owner • President • Vice-president
> Department • Facility manager

Two formidable challenges await job seekers when they call employers. The first is to get through the gates or 'screens.' Then, the second is to convince employers, when they pick up the phone, to meet.

Let's look at the first challenge, screens. When persons, especially those unknown to employers, call on the phone, they encounter verbal screens. Job seekers blocked by these devices may become frustrated with repeated rejections. This can make for lengthy job searches and leads some to accept unsuitable opportunities out of desperation.

• Phoning Employers: What is a Screen?

> *Employers Live Behind the 'Gates'*
> **SCREEN**
> Tool to determine value of interaction
> Used by employees & employers
> **QUALIFIER**
> Question asked when call is uninvited
> Assess relevance to employer's business
> **OBJECTION**
> Negative statement
> Meant to terminate communication

Employers and their employees have a legitimate need to protect themselves from invasions of privacy and from uninvited requests. A *screen* is a verbal procedure (generated electronically or by an individual) intended to sort inquiries from 'outsiders,' recognize and keep out distractions. Of course, this includes persons calling employers and employees asking for their time.

When employers and employees screen someone, they utilize qualifiers and objections. A **qualifier** is a question the employer or employee asks an inquiring outsider to ascertain whether interaction will be productive, beneficial, or relevant to company business. An **objection** is a brush-off, a negative statement, intended to politely and abruptly cut off communication. When 'screeners' introduce qualifiers and objections, job seekers must handle them effectively, even artfully, to navigate through these 'obstacles' in the road leading to the employer.

• Screeners Shield the Employer

A *screener* (sometimes called a gatekeeper) is an employee who grants or denies access to the employer. Computer-generated-answering services, receptionists, switchboard operators, secretaries, personnel administrators, and designated co-workers may be screeners.

There are two tiers of screeners. *First-level screeners* are employees (receptionists and switchboard operators) who answer incoming phone calls and direct them to the appropriate parties. Growing numbers of employers are choosing electronic-answering systems, replacing salaried operators. *Second-level screeners* (administrative assistants, secretaries, and others) usually work closely to the employer.

Job seekers must convince the screener to connect them with the employer. Be courteous, select words carefully, and give the screener a reason to open the gates. Let's look at the message to send the screener.

"Who Comes Here?"
Asks the Keeper of the Gate

Screener
Employee who judges calls

First-level Screeners Answer Company Phones
Receptionists • Switchboard operators
Computers

Second-level Screeners Work Directly for Employer
Assistants • Secretaries • Co-workers

Now Here's a 'Meaningful' Message:
Content, Clarity, and Percept

Content refers to subjects and ideas of a message, and the words chosen (by the sender) to convey them. Words, of course, convey ideas, and, they evoke images. Here, the images to put forward need be those familiar to the employer and screeners.

Whenever we refer to others by name, we employ a powerful common denominator for creating a connection or temporary bond. Use *names*, therefore, when possible. Use the screener's name, your name, names of persons and companies the screener may recognize, names of individuals you wish to reach, and names of contacts familiar to the employer. Steer the conversation so it becomes clear that the employer stands to benefit from talking to you. Speak the language of the industry. (I.e. Use jargon or buzzwords, if appropriate. But, of course, avoid coming off as contrived or artificial).

Clarity refers to how a message is delivered. Is it wordy? Obvious? Are others able to easily understand? Say what needs to be said. Be brief and to the point. If nervous, speak slowly until confident speaking at your normal rate.

Percept refers to the opinion someone forms, upon hearing a spoken message, of the orator. What kind of impression does your voice project? Does your phone call sound important and purposeful? Are you relaxed and cordial? Convey confidence and be perceived as positive, sincere, helpful, and influential.

"Ah Why Didn't You Say So--Come on In"
To Get Your Call Put Through:
USE FAMILIAR CONTENT
Names • Employer benefits
Buzzwords
DELIVER MESSAGE WITH CLARITY
Be brief • Direct
Speak slowly w/ purpose
CREATE DESIRABLE PERCEPT
Know what to say • Sound important • Confident
Relaxed • Pleasant

Keep this in mind to help make meaningful your message. When screeners answer your phone calls, treat them respectfully. Picture the screener as an ally. Here are some guidelines for handling screeners.

• Handling the First-Level Screener

When the first-level screener is a computer, be patient. Listen closely. Take notes. Often the recording provides names, extensions, titles, and other information. Write relevant data on an index card (*member profile*) or enter into an electronic file. This may prove helpful when you make repeat calls, here. (Revisit step three, *Prospecting*, Record All Calls).

> **Enchant Screeners with Names**
> **When Confronted by a Screener:**
> Introduce yourself by name
> Ask for screener's name
> Address screener by name
> Mention names familiar to employer
> Appeal for help w/ other's names
> Ask for employer by name

When you encounter an individual first-level screener, you've an opportunity.

Introduce yourself. State your name and ask politely for the screener's name.

Address the screener by name. Calmly, tell the screener you wish to speak to the employer. Ask, "Nancy, 'So-and-so' recommended Mr. Dixon (name of employer) to me. Is he in the office?"

Ask for help. Convey you've respect for the screener's time. "May I impose upon you for a moment to answer a few simple questions?" Check the employer's title. Determine the best time to reach the employer. Get direct lines and/or extensions. Request the names of those who work with the employer (assistant(s), co-workers, and boss!). Confirm the correct spelling for these names. If you've yet to acquire them, ask for the website and street addresses of the company. Also inquire about office hours and directions.

Ask to be connected with the employer. Thank screener for the help. Use name. Request politely to be connected with the employer by name.

Here's what Mary Emerson said when she called Publican Industries to speak, for the first time, with Robert Stiles:

• Mary's Conversation with a First-Level Screener

INTRODUCE YOURSELF/ASK FOR SCREENER'S NAME

Screener: "Publican Industries. May I help you?"

Mary: "Good morning, this is Mary Emerson. With whom am I speaking, please?"

Screener: "Angie Blackwell, receptionist for Publican. How may I direct your call?"

ADDRESS SCREENER BY NAME

Mary: "Hi, Angie, Hope you're well, today?"

Angie: "Fine, thanks."

Mary: "Angie, Jim Everett of Cobson Industries recommended Robert Stiles to me. Is Mr. Stiles in?"

Angie: "I'll put you through to his office. Please hold."

ASK FOR HELP

Mary: "Before you do that, Angie, would you kindly indulge me, just for a moment. I've a few simple questions about Publican?"

Angie: "I'm really busy, quickly, what can I answer for you?"

Mary: "What's Robert Stiles' title?"

Angie: "Mr. Stiles is our VP Sales."

Mary: "To whom does Mr. Stiles report?"

Angie: "He reports directly to the company president, Ed Knoll. Listen Mary, I've got other calls."

Mary: "I'll be quick. What's Publican's web address? And, who is Mr. Stiles' assistant?"

Angie: "www.Publicanind.com and Susan Darnell."

ASK TO BE CONNECTED WITH...

Mary: "Thanks, very much for your help, Angie. Would you ring Mr. Stiles' office, please?"

Angie: "Hold please."

Second-level screeners are likely to request details because they introduce callers to the employer. For instance, secretaries who perform their jobs determine who and why someone is calling, and why their boss should speak with the caller. Here are some *qualifiers* they ask.

• Qualifiers Posed by Second-Level Screeners

WHO'S CALLING?

"Who's calling, please?"

"Is Mr. Novak (employer) expecting your call?"

"Does Mr. Novak know you?"

"Will Mr. Novak recognize your name?"

"What's your association with Mr. Novak?"

WHAT'S THE PURPOSE OF THE CALL?

"Will Mr. Novak know why you're calling?"

"Why do you want to speak with Mr. Novak?"

"Why should I tell Mr. Novak you're calling?"

"What's your call in reference to?"

"What's the nature of your call?"

"Is this a business call?"

WHY SHOULD THE EMPLOYER SPEAK WITH YOU?

"Why should Mr. Novak speak with you?"

"Why should I tell Mr. Novak to speak with you?"

Remember that screeners are people, too. Occasionally, they will be abrupt, rude, or, if pushed too far, even hostile. By following a few practical steps, they may be disarmed and won over.

• Interacting with a Second-Level Screener

Greet screener by name. Attempt to establish a bond with screener #2. Greet the screener by her/his name. (You may have learned the screener's name from a previous conversation, written it on an index card, or added it to a prospective-employer profile.)

Introduce yourself. Briefly, tell the screener who is calling. If appropriate, add information in your introduction (your title, credentials, company, former employer, or location) to establish credibility. Express interest in her/him. I.e. "How are you today?" If a bit of friendly banter seems appropriate, go ahead. Be wary, however, of wasting the screener's time, especially if vocal cues tell you to come to the point.

State reason for your call. Explain why you've called. Share the name of the contact who referred the employer. If you've no referral, mention that you wish to talk with the employer about a matter of mutual interest, or pass along some helpful, but confidential, information. Be brief and avoid any reference to your job search. (Your job search is of no interest to the screener.)

State an employer benefit. Tell the screener why the employer should speak with you. Facts acquired during step three, *Prospecting*, along with a prepared *skills presentation*, arm you with *employer benefits*; information of interest to employers.

Ask for the employer by name. I.e. "Is Ms./Mr. (so-and-so) available to chat?"

If the employer is unavailable, ask what time would be best to try back. Tell the screener to expect a call from you at that time. Leave your name (not your number). Avoid leaving requests for people unfamiliar with you. Generally, busy people ignore instructions from strangers.

> *Guidelines for 1st Chat with #2 Screeners*
> **To Win Them Over:**
> Greet screener by name
> Introduce yourself
> State reason for call
> State employer benefit
> Ask for employer by name

Here's what Mary Emerson said when she was connected with Susan Darnell, Robert Stiles' secretary:

• Mary's Conversation with the Second-Level Screener

GREET SCREENER BY NAME/ INTRODUCE YOURSELF

Mary: "Good morning, Ms. Darnell. This is Mary Emerson. I design advertising for clients, here, in the D.C. area. I'm calling from Wheaton. How are you this morning?"

Susan: "Fine, thank you. What can I do for you?"

REASON FOR YOUR CALL/EMPLOYER BENEFIT

Mary: "I'm looking to reach Robert Stiles. Jim Everett of Cobson Industries,

as you may know, is a respected system analyst in our industry. Jim informed me that Mr. Stiles strives to keep abreast of sales opportunities in the D.C. area. I've some information that may help Mr. Stiles save time and, perhaps, lead to new business for Publican. I believe he may find this valuable."

ASK FOR EMPLOYER BY NAME

Mary: "Is Mr. Stiles available to chat for a minute?"

Susan: "Hold please. I'll check for you."

• Calling Back

When having to repeat efforts, use good judgment and be considerate. Two or three attempts per week are enough to convey serious intentions.

When you call back, greet the screener by name and re-introduce yourself. Tell the screener, "I'm getting back with ... (the employer)." Then ask whether the employer is available to chat. If asked, remind the screener of the reason for your call, and why the employer should speak with you. (Mention the name of the *contact* whom gave you the *referral* and state an *employer benefit*). If the employer is still unavailable, ask the screener for the best time to try again. Tell the screener to expect your call at that time. Leave your name only (no phone number).

More Chats with #2 Screeners
Hello, again:
Greet screener by name
Introduce yourself again
Say you're getting back
Ask is employer available
Remind screener of reason for your call

• Getting to the "Hard-to-Reach" Employer

Former chairman of Chrysler Corporation, from 1979 until his retirement at the end of 1992, Lee Iacocca, was considered by many of his contemporaries as among the most-widely recognized businessmen in the world. During this time, he was often questioned by journalists and others. Among the many questions, he was asked how he managed the enormous number of phone calls. He responded that he purposefully avoids callers unknown to him, until they've tried eight times! He also revealed that he prefers to deal with individuals who

A Third Attempt without Results
Ask Second-Level Screener for Help
Inquire about employer:
Available before • after regular hours
Direct • Mobile • Home phone #s
Who else works closely w/ employer?
Try:
Operator-assisted call
Mail a brief note
Send telegram • Small gift

are determined and this is how he distinguishes them. While job seekers must avoid becoming a nuisance, it's important to persist.

If you speak with a second-level screener for the third time without results, politely press the screener for help in getting through: When is the employer in the office? Can the employer be reached on a mobile phone? At home? Before or after office hours? What specific time is best to try? Your sense of urgency could pay off, but be wary of developing a reputation as a phone caller who gets the automatic "hold and disconnect." Admittedly, the line is fine between polite persistence and pushiness.

Making a Successful ETP

A little practice and job seekers become adept at getting employers to pick up the phone. What's said then determines whether they secure an interview. The **employer-telephone presentation** (ETP) is a conversation initiated by the job seeker with a prospective employer. The purpose is to arrange a job interview -- face to face. Like the *network* and *industry-contact presentations*, to make productive employer-telephone presentations, follow the *four-step formula*: *Attention-Grabber*, *Identify*, *Payoff*, and *Signoff*. (Part two, Companion, *Employer-Telephone Presentation Guide*).

Before phoning to speak with employers, script your part and practice. A prepared script allows you to control the course, even the outcome, of your conversations, with two exceptions: *qualifiers* and *objections*. When employers introduce *qualifiers* (questions to determine whether interaction will be productive, beneficial, or relevant to company business) and raise *objections* (negative statements intended to cut off communication), they present job seekers an excellent opportunity to showcase themselves.

The following examples and guidelines illustrate how to handle qualifiers and objections. This list isn't comprehensive, so you may want to add to it those you encounter.

> *Employer-Telephone Presentation*
> **Dialogue initiated by job seeker w/ employer**
> **SCRIPTED IN 4 STEPS:**
> Attention-Grabber • Identify
> Payoff • Signoff

• Qualifiers Posed by Employers

> "Would you tell me more about yourself?"
> "Are you a college graduate?"
> "How much experience do you have?"
> ("What are your qualifications?")
> "Are you presently employed?"
> "Why do you want to change employment?"
> "How long have you been unemployed?"
> "What were the circumstances when you left your last job?"
> "Why did you call us?"
> "What do you know about us?"
> "Do you have a resume?"
> "Why should I interview you?"
> "Why should I hire an outsider when I could promote one of my employees?"

• What is a Response?

Job seekers who handle qualifiers skillfully, arouse interest. Perceptive employers, those who strive to remain atop of their market segment or industry, are prepared at all times to examine talent for the purpose of acquiring outstanding staff members; especially when times are tough! To handle qualifiers, prepare responses.

A **response** is a four-part reply to a qualifier. Anticipate qualifiers, and plan responses. Responses should sound natural, not contrived. Be brief. Save details for the interview. Follow these steps:

Clarify. Before responding, make sure you understand the question. If not, restate it, then, ask the employer to confirm your understanding.

Answer. Keep it brief. Share too much information, and you may give the employer reason to end the conversation. Include a benefit. State how you helped someone gain something, or how you might help the employer.

Probe. If you expect a face-to-face meeting with the

Intensify Your Appeal

Response
4-part reply to qualifier:

CLARIFY
Comprehend qualifier?
Check your understanding

ANSWER
Keep it brief
Include benefits

PROBE
Ask employer about
Business practices • Problems

CLOSE
Ask employer to commit
to specific time

employer, inquire about the employer's organization or business. Establish rapport. Accomplish this by probing. A **probe** is a question job seekers ask the employer about her/his position, history, co-workers, business problems, needs, or hiring practices. Probes indicate interest in the employer and the employer's workplace. When you introduce probes, you stimulate the conversation. Consequently, you learn about the company and about ways you can help the employer.

Close. On occasion, some employers grasp the potential for gain, seize the opportunity, and, thus, invite you for an interview. Others may express reluctance. When they hesitate, offer to meet to discuss ways you might help ease concerns and solve problems. You may determine these with information obtained during step three, *Prospecting*; and from your probes. Ask the employer if s/he is available at a specific time.

Refer to the illustrations below to help prepare responses. (Response Blanks and sample probes, Part two, Companion; *ETP Guide*).

Mary Emerson prepared responses to qualifiers she expected to encounter. Here's one:

- **Mary's Response to "Are You a College Graduate?"**

Clarify

Is it a requirement with your company?

Answer

Yes, I am. In fact, earning my degree taught me the value of finishing what I start. I've worked hard to complete each of my assignments. As a result, I helped my former employer, Bob Hargrove, satisfy customers and increase productivity.

Probe

Where did you go to school? What educational backgrounds do your employees have? How many people work for you? What are their backgrounds? What background do you look for when you hire? How do you usually go about locating talent? When did you make your last hire? What about your department could be improved? What else?

Close

Suppose we meet to discuss ways to enhance your department's profile. Are you available Thursday afternoon at three?

Occasionally, employers urge job seekers to divulge the amount of salary they desire. This is a **salary qualifier.** The employer may ask, for example, "What salary are you seeking?" If challenged with a salary qualifier during a telephone presentation, avoid numbers and, yet, keep the matter open for negotiation. Even though it may seem the employer is interested, job seekers who announce salary requirements any time prior to an interview more often lose the opportunity. There's no sure-proof way to provide an accurate assessment of your value until you obtain a legitimate offer.

Here's how Mary responded during an *employer-telephone presentation* to a *salary qualifier*:

• **Response to "How Much are You Looking to Make?"**

Clarify

Are you asking, what salary do I want?

Answer

I'm confident I can contribute in a meaningful way to a reputable firm, and for that I expect to be fairly compensated in line with industry standards.

Probe

How do you compensate your sales representatives? What would you care to see improved or changed about your business? Would you create a position for the right person?

Close

I'd like to talk with you in person about how I might contribute to your department. Are you available tomorrow at three?

Employers may 'hurl' any of the following *objections*. This list is a short sampling only. You may want to add to it those you encounter.

• Examples of Objections

"Send me a resume."
"We have no openings."
"We're cutting back." ("We just laid off twenty people.")
"We don't hire from the outside." ("We promote from within.")
"Call personnel."
"Our industry is depressed."
"Call back later."
"We haven't hired anyone for six months." ("We're not hiring.")
"We're not looking." ("I don't need anyone now.")
"We've got plenty of candidates."
"Frankly, you're wasting your time."
"We hire college graduates only."
"I had in mind someone with more experience."

• What is a Rebuttal?

When confronted with objections, remember employers must continually solve problems to maintain profits and productivity; and businesses have to improve and expand or close. Job seekers who handle objections adeptly demonstrate preparedness, persistence, and self-confidence. Since reputable employers seek employees who possess these skills, they're likely to take a closer look at these job seekers. To handle objections, prepare rebuttals.

A *rebuttal* is a four-part counter to an objection. When spoken, an effective rebuttal demonstrates interest in the employer, neutralizes the objection, and provides the employer a reason to meet the job seeker. Rebuttals should sound natural, not contrived. They should neither sound defensive, nor antagonize the employer. Be brief, factual. Save details for the interview. Follow these steps when preparing rebuttals:

Support. Agree with the employer. Tell the employer you understand or appreciate her/his situation (you see why s/he expressed the objection). Mention that other employers (use names) told you the same thing, and what you learned from them. For example, to the objection, "We're cutting back right now," you could say, "I understand your situation. Dick Jones of Tempral Industries told me they're reducing their staff, too, because of declining revenues."

Probe. Ask the employer to share her/his opinion on some aspect of the objection. Use an expressive manner to convey that you've high re-

> ### Demonstrate Preparedness and Confidence
> #### Rebuttal
> 4-part counter to objection:
> #### SUPPORT
> Agree w/ employer
> Express understanding
> #### PROBE
> Ask for employer's opinion
> Problems • Needs • Hiring practices
> #### REVERSAL
> State opposite • Alternative of objection
> Describe how employer may benefit
> #### CLOSE
> Offer to meet to discuss benefit
> Ask employer to commit

gard for the employer's opinion. For example, if the employer tells you, "We haven't hired anyone for six months," ask, with sincerity, "Why do you suppose things are so bad?" Continue asking the employer about problems, needs, and hiring practices.

Reversal. Propose an alternative. Suggest how the employer might benefit if s/he tried a different approach.

Close. Offer to meet to discuss the benefit described in the reversal step. Suggest a specific time for a meeting.

Refer to the illustration that follows to prepare rebuttals. Here, Mary prepares a rebuttal to an anticipated objection. (Rebuttal Blanks and sample probes, Part two, Companion, *ETP Guide*).

• Mary's Rebuttal to "Send Me a Resume."

> #### Support
> I'm flattered by your interest in me, Mr. Smith. John Gray of Dicksen Industries made the same request. He told me he's received ten resumes each week during the past few weeks.
>
> #### Probe
> How many resumes have you been getting the past few weeks? When times are tough, do you get more? John Gray told me the economic slowdown has hurt his sales. Are declining sales a problem for you? Have you problems gaining new accounts?
>
> #### Reversal
> Mr. Smith, suppose we met and, as a result, you became inspired about a fresh approach to spark new sales. Under those circumstances, you may want to go ahead and meet to talk about that.
>
> #### Close
> Since my resume can't address your sales revenues, let's meet to discuss some ideas I have to attract new accounts. If you'd like, I'll bring a copy of my resume. Are you available at three tomorrow afternoon?

Here's Mary's completed script. Note the four steps. In step one, *Attention-Grabber*, she shares an abbreviated *self-description*. She mentions the individual who referred the employer. She compliments the employer and demonstrates courtesy, asking for the employer's time. She implies she can help him secure new business. Confidently, she conveys that the employer will want to learn more about her. She seeks the employer's agreement to meet at a specific time.

Step two, *Identify*, she's prepared, if asked, to inform how she may help the employer. And, if necessary, ask again for a commitment to meet.

In step three, *Payoff*, she entered abbreviated versions of her responses and rebuttals. If challenged, she's prepared to respond to qualifiers and rebut objections.

In step four, *Signoff*, she confirms that an actual opportunity exists, expresses excitement to meet the employer, repeats the day and time of their plans, and offers thanks for the employer's time and interest.

• Mary Emerson's
Employer-Telephone-Presentation Script

Attention-Grabber

Good morning, Mr. Stiles.

This is Mary Emerson calling from Wheaton. I work in the advertising field, researching, creating, and composing various print and video projects. Perhaps you're familiar with the Grayson Corporation. I believe you know Jim Everett, with Cobson Industries. Jim has named for me a few select employers likely interested in hiring results-oriented individuals. He praised Publican Industries and suggested that you, too, may be a source for valuable guidance. I hope I've caught you at a convenient time. Can you grant me a minute to chat?

Mr. Stiles, I'm looking to join a growing organization where I can bring my energy, skills, and enthusiasm to help secure new business. Given the opportunity, I'd like to tell you more about this, in person, as soon as possible.

I can be in your office Thursday at three. Is that convenient?

Identify

Benefit	Accomplishment
Secure new business	5 new projects for Grayson
Increase productivity	75% increase data entry
Save time	Met 25 consecutive deadlines
Enhance credibility	Goucher award
Persuade clients	Job offer/Grayson

When would your schedule allow for us to meet, so we can discuss this further?

Payoff

Qualifier	Response
"Are you a graduate?"	Required? Yes. Completed projects. Problems? Let's meet. Increased productivity.
"Are you employed?"	No. Dept. was in black. Problems? Let's meet. Free up your time.
"Why should I meet you?"	Excellence. Goucher Award. Enhance image. Award? Coping? Let's meet. Reduce stress.

Objection	Rebuttal
"Send a resume"	Flattered. How many? Problems? Increase revenues. Let's meet. Ways to increase sales.
"I'm not looking"	Appreciate. Others can't afford. Financial binds? Savings. Let's meet. Help grow the company's reputation.
"Call personnel"	Thanks. Backgrounds? You'd look good. Let's meet. Increase your visibility.

Signoff

Mr. Stiles, if you were convinced I could secure new business, and if you wanted, can you hire now?
Great, then I look forward to seeing you (day/time).
Thanks for your time and interest.

The *skills presentation* and the *employer-telephone-presentation* script help job seekers prepare for interacting with employers. The last part of planning shows how job seekers may manage time during the job search.

EACH SUNRISE BRINGS OPPORTUNITY FOR PROGRESS

Recall, from step two, *Organizing*, that *primary activities* (making phone presentations, corresponding with contacts and employers, and going on interviews and appointments) are actions which yield interviews and job offers. *Support activities* (getting materials and supplies, studying, reading, note making, preparing references, and scheduling daily activities) supplement the job search.

Pre-Arrange Each Day

Each day, select activities and designate specific times to perform them. If unemployed, allot six to eight hours each day to your job search. Employed job seekers need arrange for two to three hours each work day, and four to five hours on days off from work.

Make *scheduling* the last search-related activity, each day.[37] Just before quitting each afternoon or evening, schedule the next day. It may take twenty to thirty minutes to designate activities you expect to perform, each at a specific time.

List the activity and the time on a *Daily Schedule* or enter into your electronic personal-information manager. Begin with *primary activities*. Schedule these during regular working hours (9a.m.-5p.m.). Then, assign times for *support activities*. Estimate the number of telephone calls you plan to attempt, and list or enter them in the *Chat Log* (these are projections). Follow, as guides, your daily schedule and chat log as you perform activities. (Part two, Companion; *Records Project*.)

Wrap Up Each Day the Same Way

At a Desk:

Select activities to conduct the following day

DAILY SCHEDULE

List Activities • Time to conduct each

CHAT LOG

Project number of calls

List each call:

Name • Title • Company • Etc

To close each day of her job search, Mary calculated activities and times for the following day. The daily schedule and chat log (below) depict her plan for one day of her job search. She selected primary and support activities and wrote them on the daily schedule. It lists the activities she selected, and the time she plans to perform them. (For electronic method to arrange schedule, see: 'calendar-type' applications.)

• Mary's Daily Schedule

Time	Activity
7:00-8:00 A.M.	Stretch, exercise, shower
8:00-9:00	Breakfast, Dress for interview Research new leads Visit www.publicanind.com Add names to network Study "interviewing" materials Practice responses/rebuttals Check phone/tape recorder
9:00-10:00	Make calls from chat log
10:00-10:15	Break
10:15-11:30	Make calls from chat log
11:30-12:00	Letters to: Jack Davis--"Mortyn Co." Jill Packard--"Jones, Inc."
12:00-1:00	Lunch
1:00-1:45	Library
2:00-4:00	Interview at API w/Ron Frack
4:00	Playback recorded conversations Extract relevant info. / Update files Plan tomorrow's activities.

Next, Mary selected from her network file (*member profiles*) and from *prospective-employer profiles* the people and companies she planned to call on the phone. She projected the number of each type of call (*network, industry-contact, employer presentation,* and *follow-up*) for the next day. She then made entries in a blank *Chat Log*.

• Mary's Chat Log

DAY: *Friday*   DATE: *04/20/20--*

GOALS

Presentations	Number Projected	Completed
Network	*3*	☐
Industry-contact	*2*	☐
Employer-telephone	*3*	☐
Follow-up	*0*	☐

CALLS/EXCHANGES

Contact	Title	Company	Phone	E-Address	Referred By
Uncle Jim	-	-	410 555-0106	jemerson@xyzmail.com	-
Aunt Betty	-	-	410 555-0142	bthomas@abmail.net	-
Don LaSalle	Fitness Trainer	Health Spa	301 555-0178	dlasalle@anyco.net	(met @ health spa)
Ron Myers	Sales Mgr.	Finch Adv.	301 555-0153	rmyers@xyzmail.com	Kitty Weldon
John Reese	Sales Mgr.	Avco Creations	301 555-0160	jreese@anyco.com	Judy Larson (CGAA)
Betty Toller	Mktg. Dir.	Rotaine Ent.	301 555-0123	btoller@acom.org	Ross Miller (@ bank)
Jill Acker	Media Rep.	Golson Adv.	703-555-0170	jacker@xyzmail.com	Gail White (@ Cham Comm)
Ed Reese	Dir. Production	Garnett Co.	301 555-0165	ereese@xyzmail.com	Jeff Parker (@ library)

Adjusting Daily Activities

Regular planning and, then, carrying out those plans yields results. To maintain steady progress may require adjustments to one's planning. Job seekers may underestimate how much they can accomplish in one day and, thus, produce only modest results. Equally, they may overestimate how much they can do, failing to complete planned activities. Be realistic. You may have to alter the mixture of primary and support activities, and modify projections.

Consider at least half of the time you allot each day for performing *primary activities*. For instance, if you anticipate conducting search activities between nine o'clock and five (eight hours), designate four hours for making phone calls, going on interviews, and writing letters, notes, emails, etc.

If you begin at nine and complete scheduled activities by four p.m., you underestimated by one hour. In this case, schedule more activities the following day. If you seek to improve progress more rapidly, set projections (for phone calls) higher. Increase the number of phone calls growing your network, making more ETPs, and thus, obtain more interviews.

Fine-Tune Schedule to Improve Results

Plan for each day includes mix of activities:
Minimum 50% of time for primary activities
Remainder for support activities

Conclude with time remaining?

Increase activities:
More reading • Preparing
Practicing responses • Rebuttals

Seek to improve progress?

Boost primary activities:
More phone presentations

SUMMARY

In step four, *Planning*, prepare a *skills presentation*, a *script* to follow when making phone calls to employers, and a *daily schedule* to arrange activities each day. Careful planning puts these key facets of the job search under the control of the job seeker. Thus, job seekers may make steady progress along the road of responsibility and initiative. Here are a few points to reflect upon as you reach the planning step.

Before approaching employers, identify your skills. There are three types: *self-management* (personality traits), *transferable* (abilities needed to perform general tasks), and *job-related* (specific to performing the job). Proceed to prove you possess three skills of each type (nine all together). To prove your skills requires *examples*: clear and convincing descriptions of past events when you achieved something of value. Follow the four-step 'Prove It' system to construct two or three examples for each skill.

From your skills examples, extract *accomplishments*: The results of hard work, training, and planning put in measurable terms and expressed as short phrases. Select nine of your most-impressive ones. To each accomplishment, match or link an *employer benefit* (an improvement to an employer's business for which you have the capability to help make happen).

The telephone represents the quickest, most-productive avenue to job interviews. The more employers you reach by phone, the more invitations you receive. When planning phone calls, anticipate that employers will pose *qualifiers* and raise *objections*. Prepare four-part *responses* and *rebuttals*, to conquer qualifiers and counter objections. Write on one or two sheets your accomplishments, employer benefits, responses, and rebuttals. This becomes a script to guide conversations with prospective employers.

Every day, plan a productive mix of *primary* and *support activities*. Make entries in the *daily schedule* and *chat log*. Designate half the day for primary activities and schedule these during hours when most people are working (generally, 9a.m.-5p.m.). Use time left for support activities. Set realistic projections for phone calls and online exchanges.

Follow your *daily schedule* as you conduct activities. Use the *chat log* as a checklist when making calls and exchanges. Utilize the *network-presentation* and *industry-contact presentation scripts* (step three, *Prospecting*), to guide conversations with relatives, friends, acquaintances, and industry contacts. Likewise, follow your *employer-telephone-presentation script* to guide conversations with employers.

As *Planning* pays off, job seekers get interviews with reputable employers. Those identified and characterized through *Prospecting*. To secure offers of employment, however, job seekers must establish chemistry with employers. Accomplish this face to face, as you advance further along the road, during the interview.

5. INTERVIEWING
FACING EMPLOYERS

Demonstrate to employers your value in a convincing manner:

- *Prepare thoroughly for job interviews. Reveal to others the importance you place upon success.*

- *Perform to win commitments from employers.*

- *Evaluate performances. Strive for excellence.*

I f you're like most employees, you got your job because someone offered it to you. You probably were interviewed, too. In the discussion to follow, we explore the fundamentals of a successful interview.

A ***job interview*** is an in-person, face-to-face dialogue between a job seeker and an employer. Job seekers reach step five of the Gopp, Inc.™ plan, ***Interviewing***, when the employer agrees to meet to discuss employment. Think of interviewing as three activities: *preparation*, *performance*, and *evaluation*. Prepare thoroughly; perform in a polished, self-confident manner; and evaluate when the interview concludes.

> *Interviewing*
> **Three Activities Necessary to Win Over Employers**
> **PREPARATION**
> Activity before interview
> **PERFORMANCE**
> Activity during interview
> **EVALUATION**
> Activity after interview

PREPARE TO WIN

Job seekers and employers utilize the interview to determine if a working relationship is likely to succeed. Job seekers desire an understanding of what it means to work for the employer. This requires ample knowledge of the employer, company, and position. Employers hold interviews to select and hire individuals who can demonstrably solve problems and satisfy needs.

> ## Goals of Participants
> **Job seeker seeks to determine:**
> Meaning to be employee
> Via comprehension of employer • Company • Position
> **Employer seeks:**
> To solve problems • Satisfy needs
> Understand candidate for hire

What is a Commitment?

Job interviews conclude in one of three ways: (1) job seeker and employer agree to resume the dialogue later, (2) either or both decide to discontinue the dialogue, or (3) the employer offers a job. When employers give thoughtful consideration to job seekers, interviews conclude with a "commitment."

Employers express a ***commitment*** when they convey whether the job seeker is in consideration for getting the job. A commitment makes clear that dialogue will continue, that it

> ## Aim For a Commitment
> **Remark by employer indicates if job seeker in running for job:**
> Schedule further dialogue
> Terminate discussion
> Offer of employment

shall no longer continue, or that the employer intends to make an offer. A favorable form of commitment resembles a comment such as, "I'd like to schedule a follow-up meeting for next Tuesday at 3 p.m." In the sections that follow, we examine how to win a favorable commitment.

Objective: Clear and Convincing Demonstration of Value

In modern 'electronic' channels of commerce, communication reaches instantaneously to areas around the globe fueling competition. As it grows ever-more intense, employers expect additional benefits from employees who must contribute in measurable ways to organizational goals and objectives. Employers are mindful that their decisions put demands and pressures on employees to perform and produce. Therefore, they aim to determine, during the interview, that candidates are capable of steadfast job performance. Too often, job seekers fail to establish this important impression because they're unprepared.

Fewer than two percent of job seekers prepare adequately for the job interview.[38] Job seekers able to convey their strengths in terms of the employer's needs make convincing presentations. To do so, they give themselves an advantage over competing job seekers. Before each interview, prepare the information to impart to the employer. Learn about the company or business (in particular, areas in which you may help improve), the job and its requirements, and those individuals responsible for making the decision to hire. Take time to compile, arrange, and refine the information you convey. Job seekers who prepare for interviews, reveal to others the value they place upon success.

To demonstrate one's value requires fundamental, interpersonal- communication skills. There are three domains: *nonverbal*, *verbal*, and *written*.

What is Nonverbal Communication?

Sixty-five percent of the meaning we derive from interpersonal communication comes from comprehension of that which is observed, or **nonverbal signals**.[39] Physical appearance, poise, confidence, energy level, and cues, such as facial expression, all fit into the nonverbal domain. Cues associated with dress are especially important to employers. Dress appropriately. Buy quality clothing to the limits of your budget. Keep clothes clean and pressed, and shoes shined. Wear conservative, yet tasteful jewelry and accessories. It goes without saying, adequate grooming is a must. Keep hair, skin, teeth, and nails clean. Use make-up tastefully. Reputable employers ordinarily screen job seekers who they perceive ignore, or take lightly, personal hygiene.

Employers examine other important nonverbal cues. Body language reveals a great deal about the emotional state and the attitudes of an individual. Job seekers who use and interpret body language effectively, are conscious of how gestures, expressions, posture, eye contact, body movement, and distances among communicators can influence and reveal an employer's impressions.

Verbal Communication?

If nonverbal communication describes 'how' one's physical appearance impacts others, *verbal communication* refers to 'what' is said or spoken. Employers assess knowledge, skills, personality, and representations of self from what they hear job seekers say in response to their questions. They are also keenly aware of the structure, content, and relevancy of questions job seekers ask. Generally, they seek candidates for hire who exhibit strong character and come across as articulate, sensible, credible, consistent, imaginative, exciting, energetic, enthusiastic, accurate, connected, realistic, profit-minded, results-oriented, growth-inclined, team-spirited, productive, and positive.

In many ways, job seekers taking part in interviews can be compared to actors performing roles in plays. Actors are scripted and play designated parts. Each memorizes lines and is alert to the cues (movements and spoken lines) delivered by other actors. See yourself as an "actor" playing a lead role in the "job-interview play." The more familiar with your lines, the more polished and enthusiastic is your delivery, and thus; the more likely your "audience" appreciates your performance.

In this sense, prepare a script. You needn't conform to the exact wording, of course, but have ready a coherent and upbeat self-presentation. Give careful consideration to the questions

> *Verbal Communication*
> **Meaning derived from what is spoken:**
> Answers given to questions
> Questions asked
> Extraneous information shared
> **Projects • Reveals one's:**
> Knowledge • Skills • Level of interest
> Attitudes • Enthusiasm • Confidence

you ask. Be prepared to deliver well-rehearsed responses for important make-or-break kinds of questions employers frequently ask. Anticipate these questions, and then craft answers to address them clearly and directly.

The sidebar lists a few of the questions employers often ask job seekers (your cues). To prepare for these and others like them, compose responses which may only be interpreted as direct and unambiguous.

• Customary Questions Posed by Employers

> *"Mr./Ms. Job Seeker, Let Me Ask You This..."*
> "Tell me about yourself."
> "What are your strengths?" "Weaknesses?"
> "Future plans?" "Major accomplishments?"
> "What will your previous employer(s) say about you?"
> "Why do you want this position? Why here?"
> "How are you qualified for this position?"
> "What salary do you expect to be paid?"
> "Why should we hire you?"

• Categories of Employer Questions

Though job seekers may only guess about the specifics of what an employer will ask, they may assume safely that topics of query are among these six categories: early background, education, work experience, relations with others, success factors, and self-image (beliefs, attitudes, ideas, feelings, ethics, and goals).

> *Areas of Employers' Scrutiny*
> **Job seekers must demonstrate value in these areas:**
> EARLY BACKGROUND
> EDUCATION
> WORK EXPERIENCE
> RELATIONS W/OTHERS
> SUCCESS FACTORS
> SELF-IMAGE

Even though employers phrase questions differently, it's also safe to assume that the types of questions remain fairly constant.

For example:

• Sample Employer Questions

Further Examination of Job Seekers

EARLY BACKGROUND

"Tell me about your childhood and family."

"What were your interests and hobbies as a youngster?"

"How would you describe your childhood environment?"

EDUCATION

"What kind of student were you?"

"How were your grades?"

"Why didn't you do better in school?"

WORK EXPERIENCE

"Tell me about your jobs."

"Why have you changed jobs so frequently?"

"How did you get your last job?...Why did you take it?"

RELATIONS W/OTHERS

"Why are you leaving your present position?"

"What types of decisions have you been responsible for?"

"When working with others, what makes you angry?"

SUCCESS FACTORS

"What are the reasons for your success in general? ...In this field?"

"Were your performances rated?...What were your ratings?"

"How would your co-workers and supervisor describe your past performances?"

SELF IMAGE

"Describe your personality."

"What has been your biggest failure?"

"What are you not so proud of?"

• Answers Which Yield Offers

Imagine yourself and an employer playing a game of tennis. The employer serves. The ball, as it passes over the net to your side of the court, represents a question. As you make your approach, there are three possible outcomes: You could blow your shot, return the ball, or win the point making an accurate shot beyond the reach of your opponent (not returnable). Job seekers who deliver with accuracy persuasive answers, win points. Consider these guidelines to ensure that you win.

Prepare Answers. Before you interview, carefully fashion answers. Practice speaking them so you perform soundly and confidently. Accomplish this by answering questions accurately; in an upbeat, direct, and polished manner. Responses should sound natural and spontaneous.

Keep it Positive. Have something constructive to say about yourself, your colleagues, teachers, co-workers, supervisors, and others who may come up in the interview discussion. Of course, the same applies to discussions about your occupation, profession, and career field.

Be Brief. Keep answers brief, get to the point. Express one idea at a time. Avoid wordy, extraneous responses. Bear in mind, the less you say, the less opportunity the employer has to find fault.

Keep Focused. Frame conversation about career and business. Share skills, accomplishments, education, and community service. Talk of personal activities and beliefs only when they cast a favorable light. Avoid discussing salary and personal dislikes.

Highlight Employer Benefits. Whenever an opportunity arises, mention what you've done for others and how you believe you may help the employer. In effect, promote yourself in a low-key manner. (Step four, *Planning*, Employer Benefits.)

Use Examples. Fortify claims and generalizations with specific examples. Follow statements with, "I'll tell you why ..." or, "Let me share an example...." Examples support and lend credibility to claims.

Be Honest. Consider carefully what you say to employers. Diplomacy is the general rule. And, you must be believable. Concentrate upon the facts. Save exaggerations, elaborations, and 'tall tales' for social occasions. If asked a question for which you've no answer, say so. Then, determine if the employer requires an

Guidelines for Winning Answers
To gain points:
Be brief
Talk about career • Business
Politely "toot your own horn"
Tell what you've done for others
Stay positive • Avoid criticism
About yourself • Others • Jobs
Occupation • Profession • Career
Depict how you'd help employer
Describe skills • Accomplishments
Include benefits • Examples
Be honest • Diplomatic
Conclude w/ a question

answer. If so, explain that you will provide one within twenty-four hours.

Conclude with a Question. To keep the conversation flowing and balanced, finish your answers by asking a question. This helps you control the direction of the dialogue, determine that the employer understands your answer; and learn more about the employer, position, and company.

• Know the Question Game

Employers sometimes ask abrupt, straightforward questions. For instance, "What's your greatest weakness?" Such a question is a trap. It may be intended to test one's ability to field the question, or even prompt the job seeker to disclose a reason to be disqualified from consideration. In the mistaken notion you're being frank, you might reveal that a bad temper has cost you friends and even a job. The employer might conclude that s/he has a valuable insight about you and that hiring you may be risky in spite of your strengths and talents. Since you want to avoid creating a negative impression, your response must portray strengths and explain why potential problems will, in no way, hamper your performance on the job. Instead, describe a strength and represent it as a "weakness" when dealing with question traps of this sort. For instance, "Some have said I'm a workaholic, that I should spend more time relaxing." For questions which prompt you to expose weaknesses, fashion responses in a manner that portrays your strengths.

Expect Traps and Ambiguous Questions

Portray strengths only

Be certain what employer is asking before answering:

Rephrase • Clarify if necessary
Request employer to expound

Employers purposely pose questions open to various interpretations. For instance, the observation; "You seem to lack the experience to perform this job," could imply, "What do you have that someone with more experience may not have?" It may also mean, "Do you learn quickly?" When uncertain what the employer is asking, maintain poise. Remember the tennis game. Return the ball to the employer. Either rephrase or clarify the question. Make sure you understand the question by rephrasing it. In the observation above, you might ask, "Do you mean, am I a hard worker?", or "Are you asking if I'm a fast learner?" Clarify questions by requesting the employer to expound. I.e. "I'm unsure what you're asking. Would you kindly elaborate for me, please?" When certain of the question, it's possible to give a winning answer.

Let's return to Mary Emerson. She anticipated and prepared for employer questions. Note that she applies the guidelines as she designs answers.

• Mary Prepares Winning Answers

QUESTION

"What's the most-important thing you learned from school?"

ANSWER

Appreciation: For the value of hard work and determination. I gained a solid understanding that hard work and dedication play a critical role in attaining goals. Graduation represents a notable achievement helping launch my career. I plan to continue working hard in pursuit of my goals and expect many accomplishments will follow. Where did you attend school?

QUESTION

"What are you looking for in a job?...Describe your perfect job?"

ANSWER

I seek a lasting challenge, the privilege to contribute to my employer's objectives, and an opportunity to attain noteworthy achievements. For example, I accepted my last position since it represented a challenge to my newly-acquired computer skills. Among my contributions, I was able to help my former employer improve data-entry procedures and contain labor costs. As for my perfect job, I seek to remain in advertising applying my artistic talents, yet develop exceptional selling skills. I got excited, when I informed my ex-boss that I helped bring a new project to our company. Actually, I brought five new clients to Grayson during the last few months with them. I seek an environment which will provide room to grow for many years. I'm confident that this company can offer me such an opportunity. It's managed effectively, respected in the local market, and enjoys a solid reputation. Apparently, you're open to explore imaginative ideas and make positive change. I believe you met your sales projections last year, and are presently on course to improve by twelve percent. Is that right?

QUESTION

"How long have you been looking?...Why so long?"

ANSWER

My search is three months old. In that time, I've been offered two jobs. I will wait, however, in order that my next job is a proper fit. I understand that, here, employees are expected to pull their own weight and challenge themselves to exceed the company's objectives. This is the type of company I want to work for. Is my perception correct?

QUESTION

"What types of people do you like to work with?...Which do you work best with?"

ANSWER

I enjoy working with those who are enthusiastic, confident, honest, energetic, and cheerful. I know some of your co-workers are like this.
I produce at my highest levels when working among people who are positive, who take pride in, and are dedicated to their work. Let me give you an example: Dave Black, a former co-worker at Grayson, is such a person. He rarely complains and always seems excited by his work. A friend, who works for a large manufacturer, expressed a need for some professionally- designed ads. I insisted he contact Dave, and this resulted in a sizeable contract for my former employer. What qualities do you look for when selecting a new member for your department?

QUESTION

"What can you do for us that someone else can't?"

ANSWER

Here's what I can bring to ...(company name). I'm determined to see things through to completion. I completed twenty-five consecutive projects under budget and on time. I listen and take direction well. Of five former colleagues, I was selected to assist the division manager on a major, *internal-restructuring project. When I asked why I was selected, he told me because I pay attention and follow instruction well. I'm results-oriented, persistent, and money-motivated. I got my former job because I refused to accept no for an answer. I was flatly turned down when I first approached Bob Hargrove, my ex-boss. Shortly before I left Grayson, I realized I can succeed at a job in which my earnings are derived from commissions. These qualities will enable me to bring us new business and help build long-term relations with our clients. Does that make sense?*

• Categories of Job-Seeker Questions

Clearly, if 'winning answers' represent ingredients of a successful interview so are questions. From the questions job seekers ask, employers gain glimpses of their personal approach when taking charge. Pose them to employers when it's your serve. Here are three categories from which you may fashion questions.

Employers typically cut interviews short when they conclude that they dislike the candidate. Therefore, from the start of each interview, strive to establish a personal link with the employer. If you share mutual friends and interests, mention them. Consider asking about the employer's background, opinions about business, ideas, interests, hobbies, style, attitudes, values, feelings, likes, strengths, objectives, and achievements. When job seekers ask *personal questions*; i.e. "Tell me about you, Mr. Employer?" "How long have you been employed here with...?", they demonstrate interest in the employer as a person. "You'll make more friends by showing interest in others, than by trying to get them interested in you!"[40]

> *Areas for Job-Seeker's Inquiry*
> **PERSONAL QUESTIONS**
> Show genuine interest in employer
> Help gain affection • Connection
> Shape others' opinions
> **POSITION-RELATED QUESTIONS**
> Render view of position • Company
> Growth potential
> **PROBLEM-REVEALING QUESTIONS**
> Expose areas of weakness
> About employer • Company • Position

When you gain the employer's confidence, you become a serious candidate because *people hire people they like*! Phrase personal questions carefully, however, to avoid being overly familiar. And, keep them focused on business.

Pay close attention to employer responses. Listen and look for signs of interest. Detect interest through expressions of enthusiasm and body language. As long as the employer responds in a positive manner, continue asking personal questions. You're likely to learn helpful details which may not otherwise be revealed.

Establish a Link With the Employer
Compile personal questions in these areas:
Employer's background
Opinions about business
Ideas • Interests • Hobbies
Style • Attitudes • Values
Feelings • Likes • Strengths
Objectives

Position-related questions exact from the employer details about the position, company, products, services, and employees. When posed, these convey the level of interest you have in her/his organization. Also, the job opportunity may be revealed by the employer's answers. Compile questions in the following areas: history of the company and job (including previous job holders), hiring procedures, expectations and qualifications of new hires, duties and performance requirements of the job, work environment (within the department and company), anticipated growth of business, employees, products, services, market share, and potential for advancement.

Generally, perceptive employers avoid talking about personal and company weaknesses. Rarely will they offer, freely, negative information about themselves, the company, or position. However, job seekers should know about these matters to obtain a complete picture of the nature of each opportunity.

When disclosed, unfa-

Be a 'Position' Investigator
Topics for position-related questions:
History of company • Job
Hiring procedures • Expectations
Qualifications • Duties
Performance requirements
Work environment
Anticipated growth

vorable facts may give rise to concerns about the employer, company, position, and future prospects. ***Problem-revealing questions***, therefore, are inquiries intended to expose information employers strive to keep 'under wraps.' For example:

> *Discover the Drawbacks*
> **List problem-revealing questions to pose to employers:**
> Losses • Unfavorable press
> Uncomplimentary credit history
> Overabundance of customer complaints
> Internal conflict among employees
> Struggles for ownership • Reorganizations
> Law suits • Poor investments • Acquisitions
> Accidents • Investigations • Judgments
> Liens • Shrinking opportunities for growth

- "If I was privileged to receive an offer of employment from you, what, if anything, should I be concerned about?"

- "Tell me about complaints against us?"

- "What may I anticipate will be our most-pressing challenges?"

• Prepare Questions Carefully

Before each interview, craft questions thoughtfully. Phrase them, during the interview, to demonstrate knowledge of the employer, company, and interest in the job. And, over all, your value to the employer. For instance, the question; "What characteristics do the six employees in the department have in common?" indicates that you know the size of the department. Visualize yourself as an employee. Your questions then take on the tone of an insider. For example, instead of asking "Who are your competitors?" ask "Who are our competitors?" The question; "How much of the market share does the company have?" may be phrased to convey interest in the opportunity. Instead, ask, "What percentage or share of the market do we control?" (Sample lists of questions, Part two, Companion, *Interview Guide.*)

> *Select Questions Before Interview*
> **Give careful thought to phrasing**
> **Construct them to:**
> Convey interest in employer
> Demonstrate courtesy • Value
> Show grasp of employer • Company
> Project yourself as an employee
> Inquire about company • Job
> Relationships • Potential problems

Another important way employers assess job seekers is through ***written communication***; the visible representation of one's ability to manipulate and utilize data (on paper or in an electronic file) to convey ideas and information in an explicit manner. The resume is a prime example. Generally, employers look to the resume as an indicator of writing skills, clarity of thought, as well as attention to detail. Also, they may compare, for consistency, the resume with statements and assertions spoken during the interview.

What Makes a Superior Resume?

Described in this 'few-seconds advertisement' are job and education history, skills, and accomplishments. From a quick scan (ten seconds or less), the reader should be left with a favorable impression. The resume must be brief and written clearly in short, precise phrases (no long-winded verbiage).

Write your own resume. However, it may be wise to have a professional edit, then design the layout and, if necessary, print professional-quality copies. You may wish to use a computer application. Many such resume-writing programs are available and provide templates which simplify the process.

Limit the information to one page, one side only. Generally, use sans serif type (Helvetica, Univers) for body text, and serif for name, address information, and headers. Choose black type on white or off-white, sixteen or twenty-pound quality bond. Keep sections short, single space text, and leave areas of white space to separate content. Emphasize key information with bullets or comparable "flags." Keep margins even. Center and balance text, and edit thoroughly. Exceptional resumes are free of errors.

If you have a resume, compare it to Mary Emerson's. If you haven't yet written one, or if you wish to rewrite it, complete the *Self-Description* and *Skills Projects* (Part two, Companion). Refer to Mary's resume as a guide on the following page.

Mary brought her resume to her interview with Robert Stiles of Publican Industries. It outlines her experiences, skills, and accomplishments which match closely the *job description* (Step one, *Goal Setting*).

> *Guidelines for a*
> *Superior Resume*
> **WRITE YOUR OWN**
> Describe work history
> Education • Pertinent skills
> Accomplishments
> Free of errors • Brief
> One page • One side
> Attractive layout • Balanced
> Must be a 'quick read'
> Simple to understand
> Printed on quality paper

- **Mary's Resume**

MARY THERESA EMERSON
6408 Brampton Place
Wheaton, MD 20902
(home) 301-555-0100 • (mobile) 443-555-0137
(email) *mtemerson@xyzmail.com*

EDUCATION
BA Communication Arts, University of Maryland, 3.8 GPA, Resident Assistant, Board Member "SAID" (Students for Aiding the Impaired and Disabled), U of M Computer Club Scholarship (75% of cost of education)

EMPLOYMENT

June 20-- to present   **Grayson Corporation**, Silver Spring, Maryland
                           Media Services Department
Graphic Artist/Publicist for this noted provider of a complete line of advertising services. Duties include creating, composing, designing, layout, and editing print and video projects.
- Met 25 consecutive deadlines
- Contributed to 75% increase in data entry
- Helped secure 5 new clients

Jan. 20-- -June 20--   **University of Maryland**, College Park, Maryland
                           Diamondback
Multimedia Editor for the Diamondback student newspaper. Duties include: computer graphics, preparing line art, conducting research, layout, writing, editing.
- Helped increase circulation by 15%
- 2 articles published by "National College News"

HARDWARE •SOFTWARE •OPERATING SYSTEMS
Proficient with Mac/Windows: Adobe Creative Suite, InDesign, Illustrator, Photoshop, Microsoft Office

PROFESSIONAL AFFILIATIONS •AWARDS
Member American Marketing Association, mid-Atlantic region. Nominated for regional representative.
Received 20-- Goucher Award for creative graphic design. (Top 10 print advertisements recognized by the Computer Graphics Association of America, awarded annually by the Goucher Foundation)

PERSONAL
Able to travel, relocate.

Some employers may require more proof of writing ability such as written applications and tests. When presented an employment application, read carefully and write neatly. Fill all areas leaving nothing blank. Information must be accurate! For items non-related, write "n/a."

Who are References?

Job references are individuals who confirm what job seekers tell employers about their character, skills, accomplishments, work habits and employment history. References may be personal or professional. *Personal references* include relatives, friends, and acquaintances, such as; fellow members of church, synagogue, clubs, and other groups, who choose to associate or socialize with the job seeker. *Professional references* include co-workers, colleagues, supervisors, former teachers, and others with whom the job seeker has (had) a close-working or professional relationship.

Reputable employers routinely check references as part of the process of considering candidates for hire. They may ask references to confirm information in person, over the phone, online, or in writing. Therefore, references must be made aware that employers may contact them and prepared adequately to promote your candidacy.

Job References
Individuals who substantiate job seeker
PERSONAL REFERENCES
Those who mingle w/ job seeker:
Family • Friends • Acquaintances
Business associates • Church members
PROFESSIONAL REFERENCES
Those who've worked closely w/ job seeker:
Former supervisors • Co-workers • Instructors

• Selecting References

Select four to six persons (two or three *personal* and two or three *professional*) willing to confirm information about you in writing, by phone, online, or even in person. Consider persons who are influential, respectable, positive, credible, esteemed, who do not share your surname, who may know (or may know someone whom knows) the employer, and who will praise you.

> ### Choose References
> **Personal • Professional (2 or 3 of each):**
> Credible • Well-known • Responsible
> May know • Acquainted w/ employer
> Have different surname than you
> Will verify what you say to employers
> Can handle employers capably

Most people, even good friends, may be somewhat reluctant to take time from busy schedules and family. Contact each individual and request permission to include her/him among your references. Explain that doing this for you requires a little time and you can simplify the task by doing most of the work. However, they must provide information about themselves and their employment, and respond promptly to inquiries from employers. If any convey reluctance, pick someone else. When they consent, review the information about them. Here are some guidelines.

• Keep Information about References Accurate

For accuracy, check names, addresses, and phone numbers. References must provide information about their employment, including their employer's name, street and web (if applicable) addresses, phone number(s), and job title. Their personal email address may be helpful, too. Review items about them which confirm their credibility. Based on the knowledge each reference has of you; inform them, when necessary, regarding matters about you which prospective employers may seek to confirm. Inform them, also, that you need two or three sheets of their letterhead.

> ### Ensure Reference Data is Accurate
> **Get Ok From Each Reference**
> Check names • Addresses • Phone numbers
> Confirm employment information
> Review relevant matters
> Request sheets of stationery

Here's how Mary Emerson proceeded to obtain job references. She began by phoning Jim Avon who agreed to serve as her reference.

• Mary's Reference-Information Blank

REFERENCE NAME, PHONE NUMBERS, ADDRESSES

Reference (full name)	*James Richard Avon*
Home phone	*703-555-0169*
Work phone	*703-555-0154*
Mobile phone	*703-555-0159*
Home address	*14734 Jefferson Parkway 320*
City, State, Zip	*Arlington, Virginia 22103*
Email address	*jravon@xyzmail.com*

EMPLOYMENT DATA OF REFERENCE

Job Title	*Computer Analyst*
Employer	*Enhanced Computer Associates*
Address	*33109 Merryville Pike 601*
City, State, Zip	*Vienna, Virginia 22109*
Phone	*703 555-0116*
Website	*www.encomp.org/dirhr*
Notable factors	*Recognized by CGAA for outstanding achievement*

DESCRIBE YOUR RELATIONSHIP WITH THE REFERENCE

How did you meet? *On the job. Jim serviced Grayson Corporation's computers when I was employed there.*

How long have you known each other? *Two years*

Describe the nature of your relationship. *Friends, business associates. We both work with computer hardware and operating systems. We've socialized on numerous occasions.*

Describe matters that reference has witnessed. *Jim has seen various print and video projects which I designed. He can confirm that I possess these skills: persistent, resourceful, solve problems and meet deadlines.*

(Reference-Information Blanks, Part two; Companion, *Job-References Project.*)

• What to Tell References?

References can do more harm than good if unprepared to confirm your suitability for a job. Therefore, prepare your references. Supply them with information about you.

Give or send references a packet of information. Begin with a copy of your current *resume*. Include a **reference brief**, a one-page summary of your accomplishments and skills. In effect, the reference brief provides references a guide, or a prompt for communications with employers. Next, add a *list of sample questions for references, suggested responses*, and a *sample letter of reference* (page 119). Enclose a self-addressed, stamped envelope. This way, references may sign and return the letter of reference via snail mail.

> ### Inform References
> **Prepare Packet for Each With**
> Copy of current resume
> Completed reference brief
> Questions list
> Answers for them to give
> Sample letter of reference

With information taken directly from her *skills presentation* (*Planning*), Mary prepared a *reference brief* for her friend and business associate, Jim Avon, so he would have a guide when contacted by employers interested in hiring her.

• Mary's Reference Brief

JOB-SEEKER INFORMATION

Name *Mary Theresa Emerson* **Phone** *301-555-0100*
Position applying for *Sales Representative-Advertising Field*
Last employer *Grayson Corporation*
Last position *Graphic Artist/Publicist* **Last work day** *3/9/--*

Accomplishments: *"Co-managed a data-analysis project" with John Abbott. Contributed toward a "seventy-five percent increase of data entry" at Grayson. "Created two technical manuals" for Grayson's data-entry personnel. "Met twenty-five consecutive deadlines." (Indeed, you understand the pressure at Grayson to complete projects on time.) I received the "Goucher Award for creative graphics." (You saw this award. Remember, you complimented me on the layout job I did for Dan Olson.)*

Skills: *"Persistent." The project for the Bradford Group was a result of my keeping after Phil Grimm, their Budget Director.*
"Resourceful." Please tell employers about the time I helped you reach Dick Brown, the CEO of Crogn Advertising.
"Creative." The Tanbark project is an example.
"Solve problems." Please relate the time we had a glitch in the PageMaker program.
"Organize." You've seen how I keep my work space. Also, please tell employers about the meetings I organized on Wednesday evenings.
"Analyze spreadsheet data." Mention the data-analysis project we worked on simultaneously.
"Service clientele." I helped secure and service projects for the following satisfied clients of Grayson: AM Dix Company, Thilpen Industries, Cellins Enterprises, Silaf Service Company, and Jeixco, Inc.

(Reference-Brief Blanks, Part two; Companion, *Job-References Project*.)

Provide references a list of questions employers may ask them. Mary included a list of sample questions in the packet of information she sent to Jim Avon.

• Mary's Sample Questions for References

QUESTIONS BELOW FOR ALL REFERENCES

1. How long have you known *Mary Emerson*?
2. How do you know _____?
3. What's your opinion of _____?
4. Does _____ get along well with others? Give me an example.
5. Is _____ generally on time?
6. How often does _____ bring work home?
7. Why is _____ unemployed? How long has _____ been unemployed?
8. What are _____'s notable accomplishments?
9. What are _____'s outstanding attributes?
10. What are _____'s biggest weaknesses?
11. What type of work do you feel _____ would do best? Why?
12. Does _____ have any health-related problems?
13. Are you aware of any problems _____ may have that could affect her/his work? What about alcohol, drugs, or gambling?
14. Would you hire _____? Why? (Why not?)
15. What salary would you offer _____?

QUESTIONS BELOW FOR FORMER CO-WORKERS AND SUPERVISORS

16. How did you come to know *Mary Emerson*?
17. Why and when was _____ hired?
18. What was _____'s title? What were _____'s duties?
19. Did you work directly with _____?
20. Define your relationship with _____.
21. How closely was _____ supervised? How did _____ take direction?
22. Describe _____'s relationship with co-workers.
23. What are _____'s strengths? Weaknesses?
24. How would you grade _____'s work?
25. Tell me about a time you had a conflict with _____. How did _____ handle her/himself?
26. Tell me about a time when _____'s personal life interfered with her/his work.
27. How often was _____ absent from work?
28. When did _____ leave? Why? (Why does _____ wish to leave?)
29. What was _____'s salary?
30. Would you rehire _____? Why? (Why not?)

Provide references with help to make it easy for them to assist you. Give them suggested answers.

Mary gave Jim Avon a list of suggested responses (for questions 1-15)

• Mary Provides Answers for her Personal References

1. About two years.
2. Her former employer, the Grayson Corporation, is my client. I service their computer software and interacted with Mary on numerous occasions.
3. (Please provide the facts only! See #14.)
4. Yes. (Remember when you introduced me to your boss. We all went to lunch.)
5. Yes
6. Frequently. I've even discussed business with Mary, during evening hours, on a few occasions.
7. Mary's striving to advance her career. Her former employer is unable to offer her the opportunity she seeks. She left on the 9th of March, when they re-organized her department.
8. (See Reference Brief)
9. (See Reference Brief)
10. As talented as is Mary, from an artistic viewpoint, she's grown beyond a 'desk job.'
11. Mary would do her best work in the advertising field, at her own pace, by her own schedule, working with graphics and design. She's motivated by challenges and by finding ways to conquer them.
12. No.
13. No.
14. Yes. She's dependable, honest, hard-working, responsible, a team player, and she gets things done.
15. According to industry standards based on her abilities and performance.

To assist Bob Hargrove, Mary's former supervisor, in his communications with employers interested to hire her, Mary provided him a list of suggested responses.

• Suggested Responses for Bob Hargrove

16. Looking for a job, Mary phoned me shortly before she graduated from college. I rejected her at first. She called again and persuaded me to interview her.
17. She was hired because she proved to us she had the talent necessary for our Media Department, and we found her pleasant. That was June 15, 20- -.
18. Graphic Artist/Publicist. Her duties included creating, designing, and editing print and video projects.
19. Yes
20. I was her supervisor. She worked in my department, Media Services.
21. Very closely as her work was constantly scrutinized. She follows direction extremely well.
22. Excellent. Mary is a team player.
23. (For strengths-See Reference Brief). She's become restless at a desk job.
24. Mary's last performance rating eighty-five percent.
25. Over lunch we've argued which restaurant serves the best eggplant parmesan. Mary handles herself professionally at all times.
26. (You might describe the time I left work to be with my Mom in the hospital when she was in a car accident.)
27. Two or three times in two years, and for acceptable reasons.
28. 3/9. She left after we reorganized the department to pursue an opportunity we're unable to offer her.
29. (Not applicable. Please do not provide this information.)
30. Yes. She left here in good standing.

Letters of Reference

Employers may request formal business correspondence or **letters of reference** to validate in writing their impressions, the employment history, skills, and accomplishments of job seekers. Save time and project a professional image by printing them on quality paper and having them in your possession when you arrive for interviews. One way to assure these letters effectively promote you and convey accurate data is to write them yourself! You know the facts better than anyone. Here are some guidelines.

Obtain or create a template. If possible, get a few sheets of personal or business letterhead from each of your references. Or, design a reference letterhead in an electronic file. Enter at the top, center of the page, a heading: the name of the reference or company (her/his place of employment), street address, phone and fax numbers, and e-address. An inch or two from the bottom, left margin; enter a complimentary close, e.g. Sincerely, and your reference's name and title with space in between for her/his signature.

Start a new electronic file. Here; write, revise, and save letters of reference. Word them carefully. They need be easy to read, concise, upbeat, captivating, convincing, and error-free. Limit length to one page, one side. Keep dates current and facts consistent with your resume. Begin each letter with the date. Use proper business-letter format: address each letter; To Whom It Concerns. However, if any of your references knows the employer with whom you may interview, utilize an *inside address*; her/his prefix, first and last name, job title, company name, street address, city, state, and zip. In this case, this gives the letter a personal touch, thus making it more meaningful. For the salutation and body of the letter, follow the *four-step formula.*

The greeting and first paragraph, the *Attention-Grabber*: If the letter is personalized and addressed to a specific individual, use a salutation, e.g. Dear Mr. Johnson. Stir the reader's interest and establish rapport. Mention how the reference is "connected" with the reader and the reason for the letter.

Next paragraph, *Identify*: Briefly summarize the reference's credentials and experience (if appropriate). Then, highlight your skills, background, accomplishments, capabilities, and (if appropriate) past performances.

The third paragraph is the *Payoff*: Promote your candidacy. Proclaim that you will make a great employee! Describe how you helped the reference to benefit.

And, last, the *Signoff*: In the final paragraph urge the reader to seriously consider your candidacy, and to call the reference if additional information is desired.

Print finished letters on the reference's letterhead, or; paste within your electronic template, save, and print hard copy on quality paper. Send to your references via snail mail the unsigned letter(s), hand the letter(s) to them, or email to them the electronic version. They may, of course, wish to modify or rewrite your letters. If any of your references wants to write the letter, so much the better. Your version becomes a sample. Have references return to you the letters after they've signed them.

Mary composed the following letters on her computer and saved them as electronic files. She printed one onto Jim Avon's personal stationery. She attached a note asking Jim to please review, sign, and return it to her. She collected the letter and attachment, her resume, reference brief, sample questions and answers, and a self-addressed, stamped envelope. Then, she placed the items in a large envelope to mail.

The second letter of reference that follows is from Mary's former boss, Bob Hargrove. Mary discovered that he is acquainted with Robert Stiles of Publican Industries; someone with whom she desires to interview. Thus, she is able to personalize this letter. She printed on Bob's business letterhead, this letter and another addressed; To Whom It Concerns. Then, Mary sent to Bob both letters along with the same items she mailed to Jim Avon. As she did with Jim, she asked Bob to please review, sign, and return the letters to her.

Notice that the four paragraphs in the body of her letters follow the four steps: *Attention-Grabber*, *Identify*, *Payoff*, and *Signoff*.

• Mary's Letter from a Personal Reference

JAMES RICHARD AVON
14734 Jefferson Parkway #320
Arlington, VA 22103
703-555-0159
jravon@xyzmail.com

April 2, 20--

To Whom It Concerns:

Say you were offered a chance to examine for hire an 'industry gem;' someone who may help bring sparkle to your business. You'd likely seize such an opportunity, wouldn't you? A friend and business associate, Mary Theresa Emerson, has asked me to recommend her to a few selected employers. I understand she expects to parlay her talents to acquire a sales position in the advertising business, perhaps working for your company. I'm pleased to support Mary's efforts to obtain a meaningful job within the arena of sales.

I service computers and operating programs. Among my clients is Grayson Corporation, Mary's former employer. During the past two years, I interacted with Mary on a number of occasions. She has consistently performed outstanding work. She's persistent, creative, and has an excellent grasp of the technical aspects of graphic design. Her ability to meet deadlines, solve problems, and work productively with others, has helped her to be successful.

Mary will shine as a sales representative. She has a knack for making a great first impression! When I introduced her to my boss a number of months ago, he commented about hiring her to work for us. Because of her, I recommended Grayson to two clients. Later, both shared with me that my advice was, indeed, helpful. This, of course, made me look knowledgeable.

For your continued success within the advertising industry or related field, I highly recommend Mary Emerson as a sales representative. Please contact me if you think I can answer questions about Mary.

Sincerely,

James Richard Avon, Computer Analyst
Enhanced Computer Associates

• Mary's Letter from a Professional Reference

 **GRAYSON CORPORATION**
9300 Oakley Circle Suite 300
Silver Spring, Maryland 20910
(v)301.555.0122 (f)301.555.0122
www.graysoncorp.com

April 2, 20--

Mr. Robert Anderson Stiles, Jr.
Vice President, Sales
PUBLICAN INDUSTRIES
1032 Whitesford Pl.
Silver Spring, MD 20910

Dear Mr. Stiles:

You and I met, briefly, at the Ad Media International Trade Show, last November. I'm writing to call your attention to Mary Emerson, who seeks a challenging sales position in the advertising industry.

Mr. Stiles, I've been in the advertising business for twelve years and presently direct Media Services for Grayson. Mary joined my department, after graduating from the University of Maryland, and worked under me for twenty-one months. Her assignments included creating print and video advertisements. She performed her duties in an outstanding fashion, and never hesitated to the spend extra hours needed to meet deadlines.

I support Mary's decision to realign her budding career into sales. Competent, she will undoubtedly make a successful salesperson. She is exceptionally talented in the design-and-graphics segment of our business. Furthermore, she has been extremely helpful to her co-workers and influential among others as she helped bring us five new clients.

I encourage you to seriously consider Mary, should there be a suitable opportunity at Publican. She has proven to be an invaluable resource to those who utilize graphic art-and-design services. Please contact me if you need additional information.

 Respectfully,

Robert Hargrove
Director Media Services

What to Bring to the Interview?

Make a checklist of items to bring with you to the interview. The following are suggestions which you may, of course, modify to suit your needs.

Various papers, documents, and electronic files are, in effect, forms of **testimony**, or tangible substantiation of claims and representations made to the employer. If this sounds a bit "legalistic," it is. When job seekers furnish testimony, they offer evidence to prove the information is accurate. Job seekers may lessen complications or suspicion they might be misrepresenting themselves by having in their possession *letters of reference* (two or three), *thank-you letters*, *copies of performance evaluations, samples or photographs of work, transcripts, licenses, publications*, and *proof of special awards or honors* at the interview. Those who bring testimony and ably locate it at a moment's notice, demonstrate preparedness and organization.

> *Compile A List*
>
> **Include Testimony/ Documentation**
> Letters • Diplomas
> Licenses • Awards
> Favorable past evaluations
> Samples of work
>
> **Other Helpful Items:**
> Briefcase • Cards
> Resumes • Directions
> Questions • Answers
> Employer data • Reference info
> Portfolio • Note pad • Pens
> Date book • Phone
> Watch • Comb • Brushes
> Make-up • Moisturizer
> Mints • Picks • Tissues • Cash

Other items which may contribute toward a successful interview: wrist or pocket watch and briefcase. In a briefcase, carry relevant forms of testimony (including letters of reference), business or job-summary cards (step seven, *Closing*), a few copies of your resume, answers to anticipated questions, list of questions to ask the employer, prospective-employer profile or fact sheet about the company, and contact information for references. For note making; a date book, portfolio with note pad, and writing utensils. For directions and emergencies; a street map or mapquest print out, and mobile phone. To keep a fresh appearance; comb, hair brush, lint brush, make-up (for touch-ups), breath freshener, tooth picks, skin moisturizer, and handkerchief or tissues. For parking; ample cash. (Part two, Companion, *Interview Guide*; Checklist.)

Prepare for Interviews: Summary

Let's briefly review this section. Job seekers meet with employers, face to face, in a *job interview* to discuss employment. Their purpose is to gain the employer's confidence and win a favorable *'commitment'* (a remark made by the employer indicating that the job seeker is in consideration for the job). You reveal to others the importance you place upon success by preparing communications beforehand. There are three domains:

Effective *'nonverbal' communication* requires a physical image in sync and suitable with the employer. This includes appropriate clothing, a keen awareness of body language and its implications, and acceptable grooming, too.

For dynamic *'verbal' communication*; design, write, and study answers to anticipated questions. Generate a list of questions (personal, position-related, and problem-revealing) to ask employers.

For prolific *'written' communication*, carefully draft a resume. Select four to six individuals to serve as job references. They may be either personal or professional. Gather information about their employment and how others may contact them, making certain it's current and accurate. Arrange in a format easy to read such as a reference-information sheet. Prepare references to promote your candidacy. Provide them your resume, reference brief, a list of questions prospective employers may ask, along with suggested answers. Compose and accumulate signed letters of reference. Prepare a personalized letter for each prospective employer whom may be acquainted with any of your job references. Collect relevant testimony; tangible evidence i.e. performance evaluations, samples or photographs of work, etc. Write a checklist of items to bring to the interview.

When prepared for interviews, job seekers are ready to demonstrate clearly and convincingly their value to employers! To become the number one candidate, you must outshine the competition. Next we examine a "winning performance."

"I'M CANDIDATE NUMBER ONE!"

When you arrive at the property of an employer, you enter the "theater." The "play" begins as you step into the building (onto "the stage") and greet the receptionist.

Everything job seekers do and say, from the moment they step

> ### *Guidelines to Win the Interview*
> **Aim to make a favorable and lasting impression:**
>
> **'POLISH' YOUR DELIVERY**
> Practice speaking questions • Answers
> Recruit a friend to role play
>
> **THINK PUNCTUAL**
> Arrive early to allow for final prep
> Call ahead if running late
>
> **RELAX**
> Show sincere interest
> Address others by name
> Inquire about them
>
> **LISTEN INTENTLY**
> Make eye contact • Take notes
> Convey positive attitude
> Compliment • Agree • Smile
> Be polite • Enthusiastic
>
> **BE CONFIDENT**
> Erect posture • Explicit body movement
> Speak clearly • Comfortable pace • Volume

into the building until they leave, is under close scrutiny. Here, the goal is a favorable and lasting impression. To accomplish this, begin by telling yourself, "I'm the number one candidate." Repeat often.

Practice your 'Lines' (questions and answers) Repeatedly. Recall the lead-actor analogy. See yourself as an actor playing a lead role in the "job-interview play." The more familiar with your lines, the more confident and enthusiastic is your delivery, and thus; the more your audience appreciates your performance. Recruit a friend to role play questions and answers.

Arrange to Arrive Early. Allow time for observing the surroundings, adjusting your appearance, and making final mental preparations. If you may be more than a few minutes late, call ahead and inform the employer. Request a later time for the interview to be prompt.

Relax. Remember that employers are people, too.

Show Sincere Interest in Others. Address employees by name, encourage them to talk about themselves, and listen closely. Make regular eye contact. Take notes.

Project a Positive Attitude. Compliment others, act agreeably and courteously. Show enthusiasm and a noticeable smile.

Express Confidence. Keep posture erect and control body movements. Speak clearly, concisely, at a relaxed pace and moderate volume level.

Feel "At Home?"

Survey the property, study the physical environment. Ask yourself, "Do I fit in?" When you feel a 'fit' with the organization, it's natural to convince the employer that you belong. Look for things familiar to connect you with the surroundings. What's distinctive? For example, notice how the building is decorated and furnished. Colors? Textures? What's hanging on the walls? Anything striking about the furniture? Carpets? Drapes? Ornaments? The lighting? Is the room temperature comfortable? Survey the office equipment. Is it outdated? State-of-the-art? Assess company morale with a quick study of the employees. How are they dressed? What attitudes do they convey? Are people relaxed? Friendly? Frazzled?

Before the Employer Appears

As you approach the reception area, scan for a name plate, badge, or business card. Smile, greet the receptionist by name, and introduce yourself. If necessary, ask "What is your name, please?" State your business and, if appropriate, politely encourage the receptionist to talk about her/himself (business only) and the company. Then, ask for directions to the restroom. Use the restroom before you meet the employer. Check and adjust hair, nails, skin, eyes, teeth, gums, scent, breath, clothing, and jewelry. While looking in the mirror, smile and tell yourself, again, "I'm the number one candidate!"

Back in the lobby take a seat and review questions and answers until the time the interview is scheduled. Approach the receptionist and ask, "(Name), would you kindly inform (employer name) of my arrival?" Seat yourself again and continue to review questions and answers. If fifteen minutes pass uneventfully, politely inform the receptionist that you're on a tight schedule. Ask, "(Name), how long before (employer name) is ready?" Continue to review questions and answers. If thirty minutes pass, indicate that you must be on time for another appointment. Softly, request the receptionist contact the employer and ask; How much longer? If another fifteen minutes passes, still no employer, ask calmly to reschedule the interview.

Events of a Successful Interview

It's unlikely to predict with accuracy the direction, order, or outcome of an interview. However, studies of job seekers who obtained respectable offers have linked successful interviews with these events:

Show up Alone and on Time.

Establish Rapport. Demonstrate sincere interest in the employer. S/he should feel comfortable with you.

Determine the Employer's Business Needs and Objectives. Job seekers must know how they may contribute to the organization. Once rapport is established, obtain a description of the person the employer would hire to help achieve objectives, solve problems, and/or improve some aspect(s) of the business.

Provide Winning Answers. When interested, employers will ask about you. Here's where preparation and practice pay off. Make clear why the employer should hire you.

Ask Pertinent Questions. Learn about the company and the position, to understand the employee-employer relationship.

Get a Commitment. Before you leave, reach a clear understanding of the next step. Expect resistance and rejection. Provide the employer examples and rebuttals, when necessary.

> **Success-Yielding Events**
> **Derived from studies of interviews:**
> Arrive alone • On time
> Establish personal chemistry
> Determine employer's needs • Objectives
> Get description of ideal candidate
> Provide winning answers
> Ask pertinent questions
> Request commitment

• Four Steps To Win

> *The Performance Unfolds*
> **Visualize the interview in 4 steps:**
>
> *ATTENTION GRABBER*
> Establish rapport
> *IDENTIFY*
> Define employer's needs
> Ideal candidate
> *PAYOFF*
> Provide winning answers
> Define the opportunity
> *SIGNOFF*
> Summarize discussion
> Secure commitment

To understand how you may give a winning performance, think of the interview in four parts. Again, recall our *four-step formula*:

Attention-Grabber. In step one, introduce yourself and briefly state why you're there. Indicate you want to learn more about the company. Ask *personal questions* to learn about the employer. Continue asking as long as the employer remains visibly comfortable answering.

Identify. Determine what the employer perceives would improve the company. Ask the employer to describe the individual s/he would hire to accomplish this.

Payoff. During step three, both parties exchange questions and answers. As the employer asks questions, seize each opportunity. Deliver winning answers; carefully-fashioned and rehearsed lines which communicate clearly why the employer should hire you. When it's your turn, ask *position-related* and *problem-revealing questions.*

Signoff. Summarize the discussion, express interest to join the organization, and request a *commitment.* When necessary, determine if the employer has concerns. If so, address them. (Part two, Companion, *Interview Guide*).

The following illustration contains excerpts from each step of Mary Emerson's interview with Robert Stiles of Publican Industries. This is how some of the dialogue may have sounded.

• Mary Emerson's Interview Illustration

Attention-Grabber

"Good afternoon, Mr. Stiles (Eye contact, firm handshake and smile), I'm Mary Emerson. It's a pleasure to meet you. I saw the color ad for the Emory Foundation. It's a beautiful piece of work."

"I'm here today as a result of some things I've learned about Publican, and our phone conversation last Wednesday afternoon. I'd like to learn more about you and Publican Industries. I aim to determine how I can bring my energy, skills, and enthusiasm to help secure new business, increase Publican's sales revenues, and grow the company reputation."

"Mr. Stiles (People respond to their names. Use them.), let me briefly share some facts about myself. As long as I can remember, I've been creative. When I was a child, I began with art lessons. I still draw, in my spare time to keep up my 'chops.' I've worked three years in advertising, creating numerous print and video projects. To complete these projects required research, writing, illustrating, design, layout, and editing. I've a B.A.

in communication arts. I've received the Goucher Award for creative graphics. I'm a member of AMA. I created new business for my former employer, by helping bring aboard five new accounts."

"I have a few questions for you, if that's okay."

"I believe you've been in the advertising industry for fifteen years and with Publican for six. Is that correct? Tell me about your career prior to Publican. How did you come to work here? What do you do, exactly? What's your opinion of the latest Golden Ad awards? Tell me about your recent achievements..."

Identify

(Stiles) -- *"Mary, tell me more about you."*

(Mary) -- "Before I fill in the details, let me understand more about your objectives. Then, I can give you relevant information about me. Okay? Let me ask you this; What would you like to see changed, improved, or enhanced at Publican? Please describe the per-

son you would hire to accomplish this, if such a person was available?"

"Are you saying, if you found someone who could increase the sales, over the next twelve months, in the DC area, by twelve percent; you'd likely hire that person? What other requirements are important? Any others?"

"Are the company's goals different from yours? What are they?"

Payoff

(Stiles) -- *"What do you know about being a Sales Representative?"*

(Mary) -- "I'll call on advertising agencies, manufacturers, banks, trade associations, non-profit organizations, and various businesses needing graphic art services, such as layout, illustration and photography. I'll advise customers in methods of composing layouts. I'll inform customers what types of art work are available through Publican. I'll compute job costs and deliver proofs for approval and purchase. I'll maintain our existing clients and expand our client base to increase revenues. What else would you require of me to be a successful representative for Publican?"

(Stiles) -- *"Mary, tell me, what do you know about Publican?"*

(Mary) -- "It's a private company, employing sixty, founded in 1969 by Don Publick and John Candle. Annual revenues are in the area of $8 million. It has about a five-percent share of the regional market. It owns Owin Printing. Recently, a new computer system was installed to manage account administration. I might be helpful with this, since I was instrumental in helping my former employer increase, by seventy-five percent, the amount of data entered in a month. Shall I continue?"

(Stiles) – *"Please explain why you called us."*

(Mary) -- "I learned of Publican at last month's Mid-Atlantic Advertising Association Trade Show. There, I became enthralled by the quality of work displayed at your booth. I got the opinion of Jim Everett of Cobson Industries, whom I respect, and whom I believe you know, too. He speaks highly of Publican. Importantly, I seek a lasting challenge and the opportunity to develop selling skills. After speaking with current and former employees, I learned there's room for Publican to grow, and that working for Publican would enable me to develop sales skills. Does that make sense?"

(Stiles) -- *"Mary, where do you see yourself three years from now? In five years?"*

(Mary) -- "Though no fortune-teller, I do have plans. I want to be more visible in the advertising field and build a solid reputation. I expect to be with a company that provides challenging work and opportunity to assume a greater amount of responsibility. I see myself in a position, preferably here, with Publican, that best utilizes my skills and abilities. What about Publican, Mr. Stiles? Where will it be in three years?...Five years?"

(Stiles) -- *"Do you have any questions?"*

(Mary) "Yes. Can you make a hiring decision today? What's your hiring procedure? Please tell me more about this position and the people who have worked it..."

"Mr Stiles, would it be appropriate at this time to ask you a few more questions? For example, what's the biggest problem facing Publican right now...?"

Signoff

"I'd like to briefly review what we've discussed to make sure I've a clear understanding. You're responsible for Publican's sales activities and revenues. You supervise six advertising representatives who cover the mid-Atlantic region. This year, you're striving to increase revenues from sales in the DC area by twelve percent or more beyond last year's total. You seek to hire people who can help grow Publican's bottom line, enhance its reputation, and provide potential for future leadership. Is that correct?"

"I've been in advertising for three years creating print and video projects for various clients. I've written, edited, designed, illustrated, and have done layouts. I've worked closely with creative individuals and budget managers. Mr. Stiles, here's what I believe I can bring to Publican Industries: I'm determined to see things through to completion. I completed twenty-five consecutive projects under budget and on time. I listen and take direction well. At Grayson, I was selected from five colleagues to assist the division manager on a major internal-restructuring project. He told me I was selected because I listen and take direction well. I'm results-oriented, persistent, and money-motivated. I got my job with Grayson because I refused to take no for an answer. I was flatly turned down when I first approached Bob Hargrove, my ex-boss. Before I left my former employer, I realized I can be motivated by an opportunity enabling me to earn unrestricted income based upon my effort and ability."

"Others have affirmed my potential for leadership. For instance, I've been nominated to represent the AMA in this region. These qualities and accomplishments could help me bring new business to Publican, enhance our reputation, and prepare me to provide leadership, ensuring Publican's future."

"Mr. Stiles, I want to join an organization like Publican. I want to be challenged by my work and make a meaningful contribution to a reputable, growing concern."

"Based on our discussion today, how do you feel about the prospect of my becoming part of Publican Industries?" (Pause...)

"Let me address your concern about my lack of formal sales experience. One of the five new projects I helped bring to Grayson was for the Bradferd Group. They're a computer-consulting firm whose clients include banks and other financial organizations. A number of months ago, John Decker, a computer analyst who works for the Bradferd Group, was working with Jim Avon, my close friend and business associate. Mr. Decker commented about needing to do some advertising, and Jim told him about Grayson's services. Phil Grimm, Bradferd's budget director, refused to allot funds for advertising at the time. I urged Jim to invite Mr. Grimm to Grayson to determine if we could help the Bradferd Group grow its image. When Mr. Grimm came to the Media Department, I spent thirty minutes with him. During this time, I identified his needs and the areas where the Bradferd Group could use some polish on their image. I explained how I felt we could help, and showed him some examples of my work. Convinced, he granted us an opportunity, and as a result, Grayson landed a new account. Provided we both wish to continue the interview process, what would be the next step?"

"Mr. Stiles, thank you for your time, and the opportunity to learn more about Publican Industries. I look forward to meeting Mr. Knoll next Tuesday."

Ordinarily, you compete against qualified candidates every interview. For this reason, it's crucial to keep in contact with employers after the conclusion of interviews. Persistence and follow-through are traits employers recognize and want in their employees. This is an opportunity to prove that you possess these. (Step seven, *Closing*). To keep communications productive and improve effectiveness at interviewing, assess your performances. Next, we discuss the evaluation.

THERE'S ALWAYS ROOM FOR IMPROVEMENT

Evaluate each interview as soon after the conclusion as possible, while the dialogue is still fresh in your mind. An evaluation helps in subsequent communications with the employer, and in other interviews.

Assess the image you presented during the interview:

- *Nonverbal communication* involves messages which may be observed: seen, heard, smelled, and felt. Did your body language reinforce your image? Were you able to interpret what the employer conveyed through body language? Were your dress and grooming acceptable? How was your general physical image? Were you confident? Did you convey interest in others? Was your image on par with those who work in the organization?

- *Verbal communication* refers to the content and delivery of your spoken message. How was your vocabulary and grammar? Did you talk about *employer benefits*, ask pertinent *questions*, and use *names* and *examples*? How did you express your message? For instance, did you talk at a relaxed pace? Were you direct or did you ramble? Did you articulate clearly? Did you appear accurate? Agreeable? Focused?

- *Written communication* illustrates one's ability to convey ideas and information via the printed word. This is accomplished by manipulating and utilizing data (on paper or in an electronic file) in an explicit manner. Did you have with you a resume, references, and other written or electronic forms of testimony (i.e. performance evaluations, samples or photographs of work, etc.)?

Make a record of the exchange with the employer. Note topics of the discussion. Enter your impressions of the interview. These may help identify areas of your performance requiring improvement. (Part two, Companion, *Interview-Evaluation Blank*.)

Immediately after the interview with Robert Stiles of Publican Industries (while fresh in her memory), Mary performed an evaluation.

• Mary's Interview Evaluation

Interviewer/Company: *Bob Stiles/Publican*   Interview date: *4/25/--*

PERFORMANCE REVIEW

DIRECTIONS: Rate each item below. Check (✓)column 1 if you think you conveyed a refined image, column 2 for a satisfactory image, and column 3 if you need to improve.

Nonverbal Communication

	1	2	3
Body Language			
Breathing		✓	
Energy level	✓		
Expressions	✓		
Eye contact	✓		
Gestures		✓	
Handshake		✓	
Interpretation (of others')		✓	
Listening	✓		
Movement		✓	
Posture		✓	
Reinforce verbal communication			✓
Smile	✓		
Spatial relations			✓
Dress/Grooming/Hygiene			
Breath	✓		
Clothing	✓		
Hair	✓		
Nails	✓		
Scent	✓		
Skin	✓		
Teeth	✓		

General Physical Image

	1	2	3
Composure		✓	
Confidence		✓	
Interest (in others)	✓		
Poise		✓	
Punctuality	✓		
Suitability of Image	✓		

Verbal Communication

Content of Message

	1	2	3
Buzzwords		✓	
Employer Benefits		✓	
Examples	✓		
General Vocabulary	✓		
Grammar	✓		
Names		✓	
Questions	✓		

Delivery of Message

	1	2	3
Articulation		✓	
Brevity		✓	
Rate/Pace of Speech		✓	
Spontaneity/Naturalness		✓	
Volume		✓	

General Auditory Image (Did you seem...)

	1	2	3
Accurate		✓	
Agreeable	✓		
Believable/Convincing/Credible	✓		
Consistent		✓	
Courteous/Polite/Respectful	✓		
Dependable	✓		
Desirable/Likeable		✓	

	1	2	3
Enthusiastic	✓		
Focused	✓		
Hard-working	✓		
Honest	✓		
Loyal		✓	
Positive	✓		
Prepared	✓		
Profit-minded	✓		
Team-oriented		✓	

Written Communication   1   2   3

Preparation

	1	2	3
References	✓		
Resume	✓		
Testimony		✓	

CONTENT SUMMARY

DIRECTIONS: Answer the questions. If you need more space, use another sheet of paper.

Was an application required? *No* (If so, describe it.)

Did you take any written tests? *No* (If so, describe it.)

How long did the interview last? *One hour*

What did you learn about the employer you didn't know before the interview? (i.e. background, likes, strengths, items you have in common with employer, needs, goals) *Stiles is involved with trade associations; CGAA, MAAA. Knows director of Goucher Foundation. Has large family, loves to eat, fan of Redskins, graduate of Wharton School of Business, golfer. His major challenge is to improve sales management skills.*

What did you learn about the company you didn't know before the interview? *Clients include: Emory Foundation, Evergreen, Whitecap Societies.*

Who held the job last? What do you know about her/him? Why did s/he leave? *Jim Roarke. Left three months ago. Was recruited. Is now with Nu-Voh Advertising.*

List the questions the interviewer asked. *Tell me about yourself. What do you know about being a sales rep? ... About Publican? ... Why'd you call us? ... Your plans?*

Describe employer's needs. *Expand reputation, increase sales.*

Describe company objectives. *Survival through perpetual leadership.*

Describe job and potential for growth. *Territory sales management, excellent.*

What did you do or say that might detract from your image? *Perhaps too much body movement. I may have been too wordy and strayed a bit.*

What were the interviewer's concerns? How did you ease them? *No formal sales experience. I cited examples where I sold myself.*

What did you learn about the company, interviewer, and position that may be cause for concern? *They've lost a number of accounts to competition.*

Describe the next step. *Meet next Tuesday with company president.*

Notes: *Stiles recommended I spend a day in the field with Jill Brown, one of their representatives. Also, he suggested I become acquainted with their customer-service department.*

OBSERVATIONS

DIRECTIONS: Record your impressions as soon as possible after the conclusion of the interview.

Describe the image you conveyed to company employees. *Friendly, courteous, interested, professional.*

Characterize interviewer's initial reaction to you. *Professional, polite, low-key, tough, somewhat interested.*

Did you establish rapport with the interviewer? (If yes, how?) *Yes. I learned his passions and spoke about them: Family, food, and advertising.*

Which of the interviewer's questions stumped you? How did you respond? *How do you think you can help us? Why are you better than someone with formal sales experience? I explained what I could do for Publican and supported my claims with examples.*

Describe the interviewer's impressions of you. *He thinks that my character is a good fit. He expressed concern about my lack of a track record in sales.*

What are your feelings about the opportunity and the employer? *This is a terrific opportunity. Initial impression is positive.*

Did you neglect to add anything to the discussion that would have helped your chance for success? *Yes* If so, what? *I could have cited more relevant examples of my relations with others, and my organizational skills.*

What could you have improved? *Seating proximity. I could have been more relaxed. I could have reduced my use of gestures and body movement. I could have been less verbose, more direct and focused.*

What could you have done to better prepare yourself? *Devoted more time to polishing my delivery of answers and skill examples.*

Describe how you can make a positive contribution to this organization. *Help fellow employees utilize more fully the new computer system, open new accounts, and provide potential to lead company in the future.*

Your general impressions (positive and negative): *I'm excited by the thought of working here. I like Stiles and feel I could learn a lot from him.*

Additional observations:

Thus, having prepared thoroughly, performed successfully, and evaluated accurately her interviews; Mary Emerson has advanced further her position along the road to success. Via activities under her control, she has brought into view her destination; a suitable offer of employment.

SUMMARY

Step five of the SDJS, *Interviewing*, unfolds as job seekers face employers interested to hire. Both parties exchange information to learn about each other. They communicate through *nonverbal*, *verbal*, and *written* means. Job seekers engage, during the interviewing step, in three activities: *preparation*, *performance*, and *evaluation*. To carry out these productively requires an investment of time and practice. Here are a few points to keep in mind as you reach step five of the Gopp, Inc.™ project:

Prepare to meet employers. Dress and groom to match the image of those who work in similar positions for the company. Review the basics of body language (expressing and interpreting). Complete and study the *skills presentation* (Step four, *Planning*). Design and write *winning answers* to anticipated questions. Practice articulating these. List *questions* to ask employers. There are three categories: *personal*, *product-related*, and *problem-revealing*. Draft a *resume*. Select *references*. Get from them information regarding their identity and how others may contact them. Furnish references with your resume, a *reference brief*; information about you for them to give employers, and *answers* to sample questions from employers. Include pre-written *letters of reference*. Have them sign and return these to you. Make a *checklist* of the items to bring to interviews; i.e. testimony, briefcase, resume, etc. Assemble these. Job seekers convey to others their desire to get hired, via preparation.

Performance involves all that job seekers do and say in front of the employer and associates. The job seeker strives to establish a personal link and demonstrate clearly and convincingly how the employer would benefit if s/he is hired. Follow the *four-step formula*; *Attention-Grabber*, *Identify*, *Payoff*, and *Signoff* to fashion each interview into manageable sections. This provides a structure for delivering a winning performance. A *commitment* is a statement expressed by employers that describes whether the job seeker is in consideration for an offer. A successful performance concludes with a favorable commitment.

When both parties become interested in each other, communication continues after the conclusion of the interview. Evaluate each interview as soon as possible. An accurate *evaluation* helps ensure a firm grasp of pertinent topics during subsequent communication with the employer. It may also play a vital role in helping improve interview techniques.

When job seekers prepare thoroughly, deliver winning performances, and evaluate purposefully their interviews, they obtain favorable commitments when facing employers.

Each successful interview yields a job offer and leads to a discussion about compensation. In the next segment, we discuss how job seekers may advance through the negotiating step of the SDJS and emerge with an ideal employment contract.

6. NEGOTIATING
REACHING AN AGREEMENT

IN THIS CHAPTER...

Shape a meaningful agreement with your new employer:

- *Calculate needs to determine self worth. Get a firm grasp of your market value and professional image.*

- *Build upon favorable commitments. Recognize and strive for an ideal employment proposal.*

- *Make decisions which advance your career, enrich your life, and, thus, secure your future.*

When job seekers receive an offer of employment, they face an important decision. What they do then may have a lasting impact on their career and lifestyle. To get the best deal while indulging the employer requires an agreement.

Step six, in the Gopp, Inc.™ plan, **Negotiating**, is an interactive process between employer and job seeker (prospective new employee) that defines a proposed business relationship. It begins as employers discuss expectations about compensation and working conditions. The objective becomes a working relationship, to which both parties are bound; and, from which both anticipate gaining something of value.

In the following section, we examine three keys to negotiating successfully and how to attain each:

First: a realistic appraisal of self to determine *needs*. A firm grasp of needs enables job seekers to relate with confidence to employers when discussing expectations about compensation and working conditions.

> ### Negotiating
> **Process to define business relationship**
> Discuss compensation • Working conditions
> **Three keys to successful negotiating:**
> #### DEFINING NEEDS
> Helps determine self worth
> #### PRODUCING AN EMPLOYMENT PROPOSAL
> Conditions described in writing
> #### MAKING THE DECISION
> Accept • Decline • Negotiate

Second: specifics about compensation and working conditions. Putting these in writing thus, yielding an *employment proposal*.

And third: a decision. When they extend a job offer, employers generally urge candidates to accept. If an offer fails to meet expectations in some significant way, for example, if the salary is insufficient, or if important benefits are omitted; job seekers have an opportunity to improve it before deciding. They can request adjustments so it meets their expectations. An *evaluation* of each job offer may help make clear the decision.

Able to negotiate effectively, job seekers may shape a mutually-beneficial agreement with employers.

Here are three terms associated with negotiation of employment agreements.

Compensation refers to wages, benefits, and privileges employers provide employees in exchange for performance of specific duties.

> **Topics of Employment Negotiations**
> **COMPENSATION**
> Wages • Benefits
> Privileges
> **JOB OFFER**
> Expression of employer
> to hire job seeker
> **EMPLOYMENT PROPOSAL**
> Details of job offer
> Written • Printed

Job seekers receive an offer of employment, or a **job offer**, when employers express desire (in simple terms) to hire them. Offers may be extended by the spoken word or in writing. When detailed and placed in tangible form as writing or print, each becomes an **employment proposal**. Inked onto paper or saved as a digital file are provisions for job requirements, working conditions, compensation, and space for signatures.

SELF WORTH IS WORTHWHILE

Job seekers who ably negotiate generous job offers know their worth in the marketplace. How about you? Prepare by appraising your needs. There are two types.

Material needs are items which must be purchased or paid to maintain one's standard of living, i.e. rent or mortgage, food, transportation, utilities, clothing, tools, equipment, insurances, and obligations such as taxes. The combined costs for these represent a measure of self worth.

Know, also, the *market value* of the position you seek. It's another indicator of self worth. Determine how others who work in similar positions, who possess experience and talent similar to yours, are compensated. Identify and speak with them (or others who know what they earn), and/or check salary surveys. Able to communicate confidently with employers regarding self worth and market value, you establish a base from which negotiation occurs.

Career needs are conditions necessary to sustain and grow one's livelihood, i.e. nature of job responsibilities, degree of challenge, long-term goals, types of colleagues, style of work environment, and others such as continuing education. One's choices regarding these determine her/his level of ambition in the business world: Yet another indicator of self worth. Choose those which you believe reflect your professional image and may help you attain your occupational goals. Generally, these play a role in the negotiation process.

> *Ensure Confidence by Appraising Needs*
> **Material needs**
> Requirements to maintain lifestyle
> Measure of self worth
> i.e. Mortgage • Food • Utilities • Etc.
> **Career needs**
> Requirements to maintain livelihood
> Reflects ambition • Professional image
> I.e. Job responsibilities • Long-term Goals • Etc.

Below, Mary Emerson defines her *material* and *career needs*. She developed an accurate estimate of the market value for her skills and experience by doing a little research. She located and examined salary surveys online, published by professional associations in her industry, and the Bureau of Labor Statistics, U.S. Dept of Labor.[41]

Then, speaking with *industry contacts*, she learned about their compensation packages.

• Mary Emerson's Needs Inventory

MATERIAL NEEDS
Salary

Minimum you need: *$3000/mo.*   Why is this your minimum? *Living expenses. Pays basic necessities: rent, utilities, phone, car payment, gas, food, clothes, insurance, taxes.*

Income you want: *$3500-4000/mo.*   Why are you worth this amount? *Industry average for Graphic Art Sales Representatives. (Sources: AAIA Journal of Advertising, Department of Labor - Bureau of Labor Statistics, salary.com; conversations with Dean Johnson of Avco Creations, Bill Dickens of Express Printing, and Jim Roarke of NuVoh Advertising.)*

Additional Income

Do you have any?   *Yes*   If yes, amount? *$500-1,000/annum*
Is this expendable?   *Yes*   Why or why not? *Freelance jobs I'd sacrifice if required by new employer.*

Car/Allowance

Must employer furnish? *No*   If yes, why?

Insurance Benefits

Which do you need? *Health, disability, auto coverage, retirement-savings plan.*
Why? *I can't afford to lose income if I'm unable to perform my job. I'll be doing a lot of driving. I must continue saving for retirement. Employer plan would be extremely helpful.*

Must employer furnish? *Yes*   If yes, why? *Since this coverage is expensive, I need help to afford it. If the employer has a group plan and contributes, I may be able to obtain coverage.*

Additional material needs

A new car may relieve apprehension. Recently, I've had problems keeping my car running smoothly. I fear it may stall or conk out while on the job disrupting my performance. Phone, computer, printer, and new clothes for performing the job successfully.

Must employer furnish? *No*   If yes, why?

CAREER NEEDS
Responsibilities

Which do you seek? Why? *Service a large base of clients. Sell graphic-art services and supplies in a protected territory. I want to be challenged everyday by my work, and be motivated to earn commissions based upon my efforts, skills, and abilities.*

Knowledge/Skills

Which do you want to use in next job? Why? *Communication skills. I want to continue to sharpen these skills to advance my career. I also want to utilize my artistic talents to keep them fresh.*

Continuing education

Which areas? Why? *Sales training. Subscriptions to professional and trade journals. To grow my knowledge of selling and keep abreast of current developments within the industry.*

Long-term goals

Define: *Growth. I want to expand my knowledge, assume greater responsibility, become more visible, and, thus more influential within the advertising industry. I want, also, to learn more about running and managing a successful business.*

Colleagues/Clients

Describe those with whom you wish to work. Why? *Professionals who work with art and graphics. Those who take pride in their work and careers. Working among these types of people can help me make a name for myself in advertising.*

Opportunity to be innovative/creative

Important? *Yes*   Why? *These are some of my innate abilities. I wish to be rewarded based upon how successfully I apply them to build business.*

Company's image

Is a prominent
reputation important? *Yes*   Why? *To work for an organization with a respectable image is a selling point. This will lend me credibility and influence.*

Access to elite industry professionals

Important? *Yes*   Why? *This is a way to get things done because these people make the decisions. Once acquainted with the leaders of my industry, I may advance more rapidly in my field.*

A well-managed organization

Important? *Yes*   Why? *It keeps the company stable and business affairs running smoothly. It adjusts to external conditions which helps ensure the survival of the organization. This helps keep my job secure*

Work environment

Describe your ultimate: *Flexible hours, cautious supervision, help readily available when needed. Keeps pressure in check.*

Important you get it? *Yes*   Why? *To promote creativity and provide motivation to maintain a high level of productivity.*

Opportunity for advancement

Important?   *Yes*   Why? *For me to remain challenged, gratified, and motivated to attain my long-term goals (greater levels of responsibility, a larger role in running a successful business), my employer must be able to offer such opportunities.*

Beliefs/Attitudes/Ideas/Ethics

Important that your employer share yours? *Yes*   Why? *This represents the foundation of a healthy, productive, and long-term work relationship.*

Relationship with employer

Describe aspects you seek. *Open, honest, helpful, constructive, positive. I'd like for my employer to be accessible, and to supply guidance when needed.*
Importance of relationship? *To help me to feel "part of the team" and motivated to maintain a high level of productivity.*

Additional career needs

Describe: *Professional association memberships: AMA, AAIA, CGAA.*
Why do you want these needs fulfilled? *To maintain and grow my existing network, I wish to remain a member of the American Marketing Association. To enhance my professional credibility, I plan to affiliate with the American Advertising Industry Association and Computer Graphics Association.*

(Needs Inventory Blanks: Part two, Companion, *Negotiation Guide.*)

Reputable employers and their employees define relationships in writing (print). You may seek to protect your future with a signed agreement.[42] A clearly-defined *employment proposal* formalizes and clarifies mutual expectations. If the employer doesn't routinely provide employment proposals to new hires, you must negotiate for one. Let's see how job seekers may accomplish this.

HAVE IT IN WRITING

Often, employers instruct human-resources specialists, personnel representatives, recruiters, and others to negotiate compensation packages. Generally, these individuals have limited authority and must follow established guidelines when discussing wages. Unless you plan to work for them, politely redirect their inquiries about salary. Ask them about the job, company, standard employee benefits and the person to whom you report. From them, you may determine who has the say-so to finalize your compensation. This is the person with whom you want to negotiate.

Familiarize yourself with items employers may include in an employment proposal, i.e. pay and perquisites. Generally, these are negotiable. Let's examine some popular ones.

> ### Discuss Your Future with the Employer
> **Identify individual who can grant requests**
> One with budget authority
> Prospective Boss • Superior
> **Know items appearing in employment proposal**
> Pay • Perquisites
> **Expect salary qualifiers**
> Prepare responses

What of Pay?

Pay refers to income or wages employees earn. There are several types, including: salary, commissions, bonuses, reimbursement of expenses, and severance pay.

Starting salary. A fixed payment promised a new employee. It's the basis for all future raises. Explore the limits. Seek the most the employer will grant.

Commissions. Earnings based on the attainment of projected goals or targets. Usually, the amount is a percentage of the revenues or profits produced by the employee. If you receive commissions, determine how they're paid and on what the goals are based. For instance, you may be paid in the form of a "reimbursable draw" (an advance that you have to repay) and based on a "dollar quota." Request to see the records of earnings by former and present employees (minus the names of course). Able to view such recent data, you may obtain a realistic estimate of your potential income.

Bonuses, royalties and profit sharing. Funds shared with employees from company profits. Are you eligible? If so, how is your share defined and paid? Check the past record of payments.

Expenses. Costs incurred to start a new employee in the job and perform the job. Those associated with relocating may include house hunting, closing costs, moving, and cost-of-living adjustment. If you must move your residence, you need know the employer's policy regarding relocation. Does performing the job involve… travel? … entertainment of clients?…materials, supplies, equipment and clothing?

Anticipate expenses and determine who pays for them.

Severance. A lump sum of cash given selected employees (usually among executive level) when they permanently leave their jobs. If you are eligible, also determine which, if any, contingencies apply. For instance, do you receive severance pay if you… resign without giving sufficient notice of your intent? …get fired? …lose your job due to reorganization?

> *Rewards for Results*
> **Monies paid employees for job performance**
> Salary • Commissions
> Bonuses • Royalties
> Expenses • Severance

Which Perks?

Perquisites (perks) are compensatory items and inducements, i.e. employee benefits and privileges. Some come with the job, automatically. Others must be negotiated, and, thus, are awarded.

Employee benefits include personalized services, plans, and arrangements designed to help protect employees' health and life-styles. Consider health and life insurance, pension plan, car allowance, company car, stock-purchase plan, deferred-compensation plan, salary advance, employee loans, professional-counseling services, and severance plan. For working parents, day care for children and maternity leave are pertinent.

Most job seekers are interested to protect their health and their families. Therefore, they want to know about the benefits employers provide, if any. In some instances, employees share the cost of benefits. Determine if you must contribute, and if so, how much? Here are some points about employee benefits to consider:

- *Insurance* has become a significant issue with employers and employees alike. Costs for health, dental, disability, life, auto, personal liability, and other protection continue to climb. Does the employer contribute? If so… how much? …does it include family members? …are there waiting periods or other requirements?

- If the employer has a *pension* or *retirement plan*, how may you join? Does the company contribute? How so? What's the history of performance? Is there a vesting period? Are there penalties? What other details are important to know?

- Does the employer assist with transportation? Will you drive a *company car*? Get a *car allowance*? If so, for which *expenses* are you responsible?

> ### *Some Employers Grant Employee Benefits*
> **Personalized services • Plans Arrangements**
> Insurance • Pension
> Retirement • Car • Allowance
> Stock option • Purchase
> Savings • Deferred comp
> Salary advance • Loans
> Counseling • Severance plan
> Day care • Maternity leave

- Does the employer have a *stock purchase plan* or *deferred-compensation plan*? How may you become eligible? What conditions apply?

- Will the employer grant …an *advance* of salary? … a *loan*? If so…when? …which requirements, rates, and terms apply?

- Does the employer pay for *counseling*? You may require or desire to obtain legal, financial, individual, or marriage counseling.

- What about a *severance plan*? This is a defined set of conditions which engage when the employee-employer relationship is severed. It may include provisions for ownership, such as stock or other assets, and services for obtaining new employment. What are the details?

- For family members, you may need *day-care* or *elder-care* services. Does the employer assist employees with the costs and arrangements for such matters? If so, what are the details? If no, will the employer help in other ways, such as granting flexible leave?

You may be able to secure additional employee benefits such as full-line investment services or car pooling to and from work. Be certain employee benefits are defined clearly.

Some Privileges are Negotiable

Employers may grant special status or authority to employees. This enhances their professional image and enables them to stoke their performance of the job. Among such **privileges**: a prestigious job title, a convenient start date, job assistance, a company credit card, and generous advancement opportunities.

You want as many as the employer can provide. Therefore, consider these points about privileges:

> ### *Some Employers Provide Privileges*
> **Special status • Authority**
> Prestigious job title • Flexible start date
> Visible responsibilities • Job assistance
> Company credit card • Employee discount
> Hassle-free parking • Paid club / Assn. memberships
> Education • Training • Performance reviews
> Sick leave • Vacation
> Flexible work conditions • Advancement opportunities

- *Job titles* denote status. Seek the most-prestigious title the employer can grant.

- You may need some time, before starting your new job, to adjust family and personal affairs. Is the *start date* convenient? Allow enough time to de-stress, if necessary, so you start refreshed.

- Is the *job description* defined clearly? What procedures apply in the event conflicts about responsibilities arise? What effect would assuming responsibilities outside those the employer assigns have on her/his attitude toward you?... toward your pay?

- What kind of *visibility* does the job provide? Consider visibility within the company. Who will be working ...with you?... for you? Can the employer help you become more visible within ... the company?... the industry?... your community? If so, perhaps s/he will explain how?

- If issued a *company credit card*, what are your responsibilities? For what are you liable?

- Are you eligible for *discounts* on company products or services? If so, what are the details?

- Parking may be a hassle. If so, can the employer grant special status such as a *permit*? When conflicts arise, how are they resolved?

- If you're a member of, or wish to join, a professional association, does the employer pay or contribute to the cost ...of *membership*?... for subscriptions to trade journals, other helpful literature, or even online services?

- Does the employer provide for *skills training*? Will s/he assist with the costs of *continuing education*? How will additional education or credentials affect your position and pay?

- Does the employer provide recreational facilities or membership to a fitness club? If so, what procedures apply?

- Does the employer *review performance*? Yes? How often? Who conducts the reviews? What procedures apply? On what are they based? How does an acceptable or a superior review affect your pay and status?

- What are the details regarding *vacations*, *holidays*, *sick leave*, lunch or other breaks? How do these apply?

- What kind of *working conditions* do you anticipate? Could you work from home? Is the work schedule flexible? When can you take time off? Are you assigned a personal work space? If yes, could it be improved or changed, if needed? If no, yet one may be helpful, can you obtain one?

- What opportunities are available for *advancement*? What's the next level? How does the employer depict your advancement in the organization?

You may be able to secure additional privileges such as permission to use the company's credit line, tools, or equipment. Make sure privileges are defined clearly.

Next, expect inquiries about salary requirements. When employers become interested to hire a candidate, they need determine how much it will cost them.

Beware of Salary Qualifiers!

We defined *salary qualifiers* as employer questions intended to prod job seekers to divulge the amount of salary they desire. Employers use salary qualifiers to assess the candidate's perception of self worth, and to determine that they can enter into salary negotiations able to afford to make an attractive offer.

> *Sample Salary Qualifiers*
> **Expect queries like these:**
> "What kind of salary do you expect?"
> "What's the lowest salary you'll accept?"
> "What salary are you worth?"
> "How much did (do) you make in your last (present) job?"
> "Our policy is to start everyone in this position at the same salary. That's okay with you, right?"

• Avoid Discussing Amount of Salary Until –

When employers ask about your salary requirements, it's natural to assume they're interested in hiring you. Nevertheless, it's generally a good idea to delay discussions of salary until you have a firm job offer with expectations clearly defined.

To understand why you should refuse to discuss salary prior to securing an employment proposal, let's look at what happens when job seekers discuss salary prematurely.

First, say the employer has the position budgeted for a salary in the range of $45-50,000. The job seeker asks for a salary of $52,000. Here, the job seeker overstates worth. Thus, s/he risks losing a possible offer.

The second possibility is to underestimate one's value. In the instance above, if the job seeker requests $42,000, s/he understates worth to the employer. The result: doubt or concern on part of the employer.

The third scenario is to suggest pay in line with what the employer has in mind. Again, in the instance above, say the job seeker desires $50,000.

Even if $50,000 represents more than you may need, by agreeing, the salary negotiations are concluded. Later, you find that, to perform the job, expenses and other costs must come from your pocket thereby diminishing the amount of income you bring home. Thus, a $50,000 salary, may actually yield thousands less! And remember, your income shrinks substantially as taxes are extracted.

Should you discuss salary prematurely, you risk pricing yourself out of an offer if you overstate or understate your value. Employers are wary of hiring job seekers who have unrealistic perceptions of self worth. If you indicate

> *Wait Before You Discuss Money*
> **Outcomes from discussing salary prematurely:**
> Overstate • Understate worth
> Estimate in line w/employer
> **If over• underestimate**
> Risk pricing self out of job
> **Agree w/employer**
> Concludes negotiations
> **Delay discussions**
> Until you've locked down a firm offer
> W/ clearly-defined expectations
> Preserves opportunity to negotiate
> Employer may offer more than anticipated

you'd accept a salary in line with the employer's perception of your worth, you surrender the opportunity to negotiate higher pay.

By delaying salary discussions until after you have a written offer, and before you sign, you protect the opportunity to negotiate. This way, you engage the employer in negotiations, and may persuade the employer to offer a higher salary than s/he anticipated. When you do, you're likely to gain respect and enhance your professional image. Thus, salary negotiations begin when -- an employer presents an employment proposal.

• Handle Salary Qualifiers with Prepared Responses

When job seekers handle salary qualifiers skillfully, they earn respect from reputable employers and expose those unauthorized or unprepared to conclude negotiations successfully. Anticipate salary qualifiers and prepare responses. (Step four, *Planning*; What is a Response?) Follow the *four-part reply:*

Clarify. Be sure you understand what the employer is asking. If not, restate the question.

Answer. Inform the employer that you seek a suitable opportunity and a long-term association. Express your desire to learn more about the job. Avoid references to dollar amounts, what you think you should be paid, and what you were previously paid. Stress interest in the opportunity to work for the employer, not the money.

> *Prepare Responses to Salary Qualifiers*
> **Responses are 4 steps:**
> **CLARIFY**
> Understand the question?
> If uncertain, restate the question
> **ANSWER**
> Your interest is 'suitable opportunity'
> Avoid specific dollar amounts
> **PROBE**
> Learn more about opportunity
> Ask about employer • Company
> Position (negative aspects)
> **CLOSE**
> Ask for salary range of position

When you present in this fashion, you encourage reputable employers to make reasonable offers.

Probe. Ask for details about the employer, the company, and position. Learn more about the opportunity -- especially the negative aspects! (This moment represents the job seeker's best opportunity before taking a new job, to learn the negatives or reasons for concerns linked to the organization. Part two, Companion, *Interview Guide*; Problem-Revealing Questions).

Close. Ask the employer about the salary range. When revealed, this indicates the dollar value the employer places on the position.

Refer to the following sample illustration as you fashion responses. Here's one of Mary Emerson's prepared responses to expected salary qualifiers:

• Mary's Response to "What's the Least You'll Accept?"

Clarify

Are you asking me for a number?

Answer

I'm most interested in a suitable position and a long-term association. I'll accept appropriate pay for someone with my qualifications, abilities, and potential to perform this job successfully. I wish to understand more about this opportunity.

Probe

Tell me more about the job. Why is it vacant? What problems have been associated with this position? Please elaborate. What else? What did the last employee in this job earn? Is that consistent with the industry?

Close

What's your salary range for this position?

(Response Blanks, Part two, Companion, *Employer-Telephone-Presentation Guide*.)

Often, employers attempt to bypass negotiations and 'trap' job seekers. For example, an employer may say, "We're paying a salary in the $35-40,000 range." Then ask, "Is that okay with you?" If this happens, delay your response. Let your silence convey you're aware of this trap. If the employer presses the issue, respond with a probe, such as, "Would you pay more to hire the best person for this position?"

Four Steps to an Employment Proposal

To obtain a respectable employment proposal, think of the negotiation process in four parts. When the employer talks salary, follow *the four-step formula*.

In step one, *Attention-Grabber*, confirm the employer considers you a serious candidate.

During the second step, *Identify*, indicate interest by requesting written confirmation of discussions with the employer. If the employer refuses, offer to put the discussions in writing.

The third step, *Payoff*, inquire about benefits and privileges. Remember; however, avoid committing to a salary figure or range.

> *Focus Upon an Employment Proposal in 4 Steps:*
> **Attention-Grabber**
> Confirm your candidacy
> **Identify**
> Verbalize interest
> Request written confirmation
> **Payoff**
> Discuss benefits • Privileges
> Avoid mentioning numbers
> **Signoff**
> Summarize discussion
> Describe plans to proceed

Finally comes the fourth step, *Signoff*. Summarize the discussion and indicate how you plan to proceed. (Although they are listed in sequence, the events of effective negotiation may actually occur in any order.)

The illustration below shows how Mary Emerson obtained an employment proposal from Robert Stiles of Publican Industries. When Stiles expressed interest to hire Mary, here's what followed.

• Mary Emerson's Negotiation Illustration

Attention-Grabber

"Mr. Stiles, I'm interested in salary. However, I'm more interested in the challenges this job offers. When we agree that I'm the person for the job, I'm confident we'll also agree on the salary. Am I the person for this job?"

"I want to be certain I understand this job. I'll be servicing and opening accounts in territory A. Is that correct? What other things are important to superior job performance?"

"I look forward to beginning work. I'm eager to make a long-term commitment to you and the job."

Identify

"I'd prefer we formalize our discussion with a written proposal. Is that your procedure? I ask because I think it best that we clearly define our professional relationship. Also, I'm reluctant to refuse other offers without written assurance that I'm being offered this job."

Payoff

(See Mary's response to "What's the Least You'll Accept?")

"What standard benefits and privileges do employees receive at Publican? Are there any others? Would you be open to discuss a few items you haven't mentioned? For example, would the company provide for a membership with AMA? … with…?"

Signoff

"Let's summarize what we've discussed. I'll assume the title Advertising Representative. My responsibilities include selling and servicing established and prospective accounts in Montgomery and PG Counties, and in DC. I'm compensated with a base salary, commissions, fifty percent of the cost of my health-care insurance, allowance for automobile; mileage reimbursement, paid sick leave, and a month's salary in advance. Is that right?"

"Since this is a most-important decision, I'd like to review the offer when I receive the proposal. I'll get back with you within twenty-four to forty-eight hours. How does that sound?" "Thanks again for expressing your confidence in me."

(For additional details negotiating an employment proposal, Part two, Companion; *Negotiation Guide.*)

Robert Stiles presented Mary with the following employment proposal. Items 3 through 8 describe compensation offered to Mary.

• Mary Emerson's Employment Proposal

PUBLICAN INDUSTRIES, INC.
1032 Whitesford Place
Silver Spring, MD 20910
(voice) 301-555-0147 • (fax) 301-555-0187
www.publicanind.com

EMPLOYMENT AGREEMENT

1.   PARTIES TO CONTRACT. This contract is between Publican Industries (employer) and Mary Theresa Emerson (employee).

2.   TERM OF CONTRACT. This contract is effective one year, beginning June 1, 20-

3.   BASE SALARY.

     A.   Employer shall pay the employee $33,000 in equal installments on the 1st and 15th days of each month.

     B.   Employer shall conduct a review of the employee's performance after a six-month period for the purpose of maintaining the salary with industry standards.

4.   COMMISSION. The employee shall be paid commissions based on the following formula: Five percent of profits from net sales.

5.   JOB TITLE, DUTIES AND RESPONSIBILITIES. The position of Advertising Representative shall be responsible for sales and service of all established and prospective clients in territory A. This includes Maryland counties of Montgomery and Prince Georges; and Washington, D.C. Reports to VP Sales.

6.   VACATION. The employee shall receive, annually, seven days paid vacation.

7.   EMPLOYEE BENEFITS. The employee shall receive the following benefits:

     50% paid individual health coverage or equivalent reimbursement car allowance of $200/month, reimbursement of documented business expenses.

8.   ADDITIONAL PERKS. Three days paid sick leave. Salary advance equal to one month of pay.

9.   TERMINATION. Either party may terminate this agreement with not less than fourteen days written notice.

Agreed to:
Robert Anderson Stiles, Employer   Signature_____
     Date   _____

Mary Theresa Emerson, Employee   Signature_____
     Date   _____

When presented an employment proposal, job seekers may take one of three avenues. Accept, reject, or attempt to change it. Hasty decisions to accept have often resulted in a mismatch proving costly to both parties.

On the other hand, a swift decision to reject may also be costly. Job seekers may neglect an opportunity to shape a seemingly-deficient offer into an acceptable one, yielding only regret. Let's consider what's involved in making this decision.

YOU DESERVE EVERYTHING YOU GET

To ensure you select the right one for the right reasons, evaluate each employment proposal. The more you know about the employer, job, and conditions of employment, the simpler your decision. A substantial offer clearly defines the (proposed) employee-employer relationship. It contains the most pay and perks the employer can reasonably offer, and describes job duties and responsibilities. The offer should depict a productive work environment and your place in it at the start of employment. Also, it should project your position six months to a year down the road.

Evaluate Offers Carefully
A Generous Job Offer
Clearly defines job • Objectives
Employee-employer relationship
Describes work environment • Anticipated support
Projects status 6-12 months in future
Includes ample pay • Substantial perks

Analyze all offers. Compare when you have more than one. When you complete an evaluation, you may feel confident about your decision: A career move which initiates or declines a potentially-lengthy and challenging relationship.

Assess the would-be income and perks. Rate the job duties and responsibilities. How close a fit is the job description? For example, do the proposed responsibilities match your skills and talents? Has the employer defined clearly what s/he wants you to accomplish? Is the employer's estimation of your performance realistic? Are you likely to achieve the results expected of you? Does the offer specify ways to measure your performance? Have you the necessary authority to produce the anticipated results? Does the job represent a lasting challenge? If the job requires travel, are the conditions outlined? How many hours a day does the employer expect you to work?

Focus on the working conditions and future opportunities. Rate the support you anticipate from the organization as defined by the job offer. Ample support (i.e. productive assistants, well-informed and equipped technical staff, effective inter-company communication, etc.) may be necessary for you to achieve results.

After receiving the employment proposal from Publican Industries, Mary evaluated it. The following is her evaluation.

• Mary Emerson's Job-Offer Evaluation

Company name: *Publican Industries*
Job title: *Advertising Representative*
Date of offer: *May 10, 20--*

DIRECTIONS: Rate each item on a scale of 0-5 (5 being the highest level). In column A, rate the level of importance to you. In column B, rate the level at which the offer satisfies your need for the item. Then multiply column A by column B and place that figure in column C. (Add the numbers in Column C. Use your total points to compare offers).

Pay/Benefits	A	x	B	=	C
Salary	5	x	3	=	15
Commissions	5	x	4	=	20
Bonus	2	x	0	=	0
Review	4	x	5	=	20
Benefits	5	x	4	=	20

Additional items:

	A	x	B	=	C
Salary advance	3	x	4	=	12
Car allowance	5	x	3	=	15

Duties/Responsibilities

	A	x	B	=	C
Job title	5	x	5	=	25
Job description	5	x	3	=	15
Power/Authority	4	x	4	=	16
Challenge	3	x	3	=	9
Travel	2	x	1	=	2
Hours	2	x	1	=	2

Environment

	A	x	B	=	C
Opportunity for innovation	5	x	2	=	10
Chances of advancement	4	x	1	=	4
Stability	4	x	1	=	4
Company reputation	4	x	2	=	8
Commute	2	x	5	=	10
Perceived pressure	4	x	2	=	8
Office atmosphere	4	x	1	=	4
Anticipated support	5	x	1	=	5
Personal visibility	5	x	5	=	25
Flexibility	4	x	3	=	12

Additional items:

	A	x	B	=	C
_____	__	x	__	=	__
_____	__	x	__	=	__

Total Points 261

(Part two, Companion, *Negotiation Guide*; Job-Offer Evaluation blank.)

Negotiation: The Avenue to an Ideal Offer

Employers seldom offer the maximum compensation they can afford, at first. Many job seekers, however, eagerly accept an opening offer and forfeit their opportunity to negotiate. Once employees, they are bound by company policies and procedures. You have leverage until accepting an offer -- during the **engagement period**: from the minute when the employer makes an offer, to the moment the job seeker signs -- at which time you become an employee. Job seekers who utilize leverage can attain ideal compensation.

It pays to negotiate. The compensation you accept affects your emotional status, image, lifestyle, and future. Negotiate a superior compensation package to ensure emotional stability will last. It provides motivation to keep abilities sharp as you perform the job every day. You may enhance your professional image and gain respect from colleagues. More often, professionals respected in their field get chosen to advance. Since compensation helps defray living expenses, your lifestyle may improve. And, since your compensation package will become a reference point for promotions and other job offers, your future prospects may grow. The more you get now, the greater your career and earnings potential.

Negotiate During Engagement Period

First offer is seldom best deal

Utilize leverage to attain "ideal" offer:

Maximum compensation
Enduring satisfaction
Continuous motivation
Enhanced professional image
Respect of colleagues
Opportunity to advance
Comfortable lifestyle
Foundation for bright future

• Enhancing a Job Offer

After evaluating an employment proposal, redefine and rewrite parts to understand it firmly and to sweeten the offer. This involves asking the employer to accept a revised version. Consider these steps to rewrite an offer:

Item. Choose the item(s) (pay and perks) you want altered or added to the offer.

Current Offer. List the item as the employer offered it.

Desired Status. Think of the item as you would prefer it. Be realistic. Leave room for the employer to negotiate. Jot that down.

Reason(s) For Change. Note one or two reasons why you want to change the offer. Identify present and/or potential problems related to the employer's business or to your performing the job. Think of specific examples to substantiate the consequences of the problem or potential effect, if the item remains unchanged. Note these.

Result(s) Of Change. Anticipate outcome(s) assuming the employer makes your proposed change(s) to the offer. Describe how the change(s) may resolve problems, reduce the potential for problems, or offer the employer other distinct advantages. (These represent reasons why the employer should grant your requests.) Write these down.

When you show the employer how s/he may benefit by granting your requests, you provide a preview of your abilities to perform the job. Skillful negotiating may be indicative of success in the job.

Publican Industries provides no company vehicles. So, Mary must use her car to perform the job. However, Bob Stiles' offer included $200/month allowance for transportation. After evaluating the offer, Mary decided to request a larger allowance. Prior to accepting or rejecting the offer, she negotiated for a $100/month increase in the car allowance.

Guidelines to Rewrite an Offer

Item
Identify each item you wish changed

Current offer
List the way it was offered

Desired status
List how you prefer it

Reasons for change
Write reasons to change offer

Results of change
Describe gain employer may receive

• Mary Prepares to Request a Larger Allowance

> ### *ITEM*
> #### *Car Allowance*
>
> **Current Offer:** *$200 per month*
> **Desired Status:** *$325 per month*
> **Reason(s) For Change:** *To keep my 8-year-old car operating smoothly may divert my attention from the job. For example; Monday, I was driving.... If my time on the job and focus are disrupted, my productivity may be diminished.*
>
> **Result(s) Of Change:** *I could afford a new car. This would help ensure that my work schedule remains uninterrupted. Furthermore, I may anticipate achieving my intended results and a high-level of productivity. Also, a larger allowance gives the company a larger tax deduction.*

• Obtaining Your Best Deal

When you finish writing a counter-proposal, contact the employer and, either via the phone or face-to-face, request the changes you want in the offer. Begin your request by reassuring the employer of your desire to *accept* the job offer and start to work.

Next, explain politely that you wish to *change* the offer. Tell the employer your change(s) should benefit both of you.

Briefly *review* the offer. Focus only on the item(s) you want to change. One at a time, describe each change you want.

State the *reason(s)* for requesting each change. Describe potential problems, if left unchanged. Use examples if appropriate.

Describe anticipated *result* of the change(s). Relate how your change(s) may solve problems, reduce the possibility for future difficulties, and offer the

> *Guidelines for Requesting Change*
> **Contact • Reassure employer**
> Express desire to accept offer
> Review current offer
> **Take each item separately**
> Describe desired status
> State reason for change(s)
> Relate result of change(s)
> Ask for agreement
> **Employer may:**
> Need time to decide
> Grant your request
> Refuse your request

employer other benefits. Repeat the process for all items you want changed or added.

Ask the employer for his or her agreement. This returns the ball to the employer's court and elicits a response. The employer may require time to make a decision, grant your request, or refuse to consider your request. If the employer needs time to make a decision, determine when you may expect an answer. Make arrangements to communicate at that time.

Employment Contract: A Bilateral Agreement

When the employer grants your request, or when you both compromise on the provisions of the offer, ask for a new employment proposal that incorporates those revisions. Make sure each employment proposal you receive (or write) includes every item of importance discussed with the employer. Understand all terms before you sign. If you decide to accept, sign the proposal. After the employer has also signed, the employment proposal becomes your *employment contract*. Some employment proposals overflow from excessive details rendering them indistinguishable to lay persons. If you receive such a proposal, it may be wise to obtain legal counsel before signing.

> *Putting on the Final Touches*
> **Before signing ensure proposal:**
> Includes all items discussed
> Is clear • Understandable
> Signed proposal becomes employment contract

With an offer "in hand," it's likely you experience a boost in confidence. Take advantage, at this time, to negotiate simultaneously with a number of employers. Keep your job search at full speed until you exhaust all possibilities, sign a suitable offer, and begin working.

Some Employers Refuse to Negotiate

The employer may simply tell you the offer is a "take-it-or-leave-it" proposition. If this happens, recognize the employer's good judgment, express appreciation, and politely request time to decide. Take a few days, if needed, to weigh the pros and cons of accepting a job offer that may be deficient. Remember, however, employers who refuse to negotiate during the *engagement period*, may be unintentionally disclosing their normal operating procedure. Should they utilize this tactic repeatedly and you make a similar request as an employee at a later time; that too may be handled in the same fashion.

SUMMARY

Employers, upon extending offers of employment, seldom grant the maximum compensation.

Occasionally Employers Don't Reconsider

If you wind up w/ this scenario:
Thank employer for confidence in you
Request time to make decision
Consider employers who refuse now may reject similar requests later

Therefore, job seekers often must negotiate to obtain an ideal job offer. In step six of the SDJS, *Negotiating*, job seekers discuss with employers working conditions and *compensation*. The objective is to shape a long-term business agreement. To prepare, job seekers define their *needs* and determine their *market value*. They review *pay* and *perks*; the items which may appear in a job offer. They carefully craft *responses* to anticipated *salary qualifiers*. They receive, evaluate, and, when necessary, rewrite to enhance employment proposals. They conclude by signing an employment contract.

A firm grasp of *needs* (*material* and *career*) helps job seekers convince employers of their worth and portray a professional image. Ultimately, the wages, benefits, and privileges (compensation) they accept, become valid indicators of their market value. Generally, these items are negotiable and employers have different ideas about which and how much they will grant. Keep in mind, you deserve everything you get! When you ably handle questions regarding compensation, you earn respect, and, thus, encourage employers to make respectable offers.

When presented an offer by word of mouth, express appreciation and politely steer discussion toward putting it in writing. Deflect attempts to have you accept a specific salary or range by replying with carefully-crafted *responses* to anticipated *salary qualifiers*. When fashioning your responses, follow the four-part reply; *Clarify*, *Answer*, *Probe*, and *Close*.

A formal job offer or employment proposal defines clearly, in writing, key conditions of employment including duties, expectations, pay, benefits, privileges, etc. Follow the four-step formula; *Attention-Grabber*, *Identify*, *Payoff*, and *Signoff*, to obtain an employment proposal. Upon receiving a written or printed proposal, request time to examine the provisions (three days is customary).

If the offer is a spoken promise only, summarize discussions with the employer in writing. Your written summary becomes an employment proposal.

Evaluate each *employment proposal*. Discuss changes with the employer during the *engagement period* before accepting or rejecting. Reassure the employer that you wish to go to work without delay, and plan to remain committed for many years to help ensure the company's success. If an offer needs modification or improvement, utilize the guidelines for an ideal offer to show how the employer may benefit by granting your requests. Skillful negotiating may be indicative of success in the job. Make certain the employer incorporates revisions, upon granting any clarifications or enhancements, and, then, signs the proposal. When you decide to accept and sign the proposal, you reach an important agreement with your new employer.

The next segment marks the final stretch of the road to success, examining ways to keep communication productive.

7. CLOSING

STRENGTHENING RELATIONSHIPS

IN THIS CHAPTER...

Build rapport with contacts and employers. Facilitate your progress:

- *Correspond to remain linked and influence others.*

- *Use the telephone to get results quickly. Keep the search under your control.*

- *Notate communications to chronicle and measure progress. Keep your focus upon a meaningful job with a reputable employer!*

Your project for our imaginary company is about to come to a close, appropriately, with the seventh and final step, *Closing*. The "c" in the Gopp, Inc.™ plan. You launched the SDJS with *Goal Setting*, followed by *Organizing*, *Prospecting*, *Planning* and *Interviewing*. Then, you took on *Negotiating*. At this stage, you presumably have been working each day at growing a network of contacts and prospective employers. In this section, I demonstrate how to develop helpful relationships with those in your network.

The term ***closing*** is interchangeable with asking. To 'close' is to ask for someone's opinion, agreement, permission, or approval. When job seekers 'close' contacts and employers, having established rapport, they seek to get from them -- information, decisions, and commitments. And, with these come leads, interviews, and job offers.

In step three, *Prospecting*, we examine and provide illustrations of the conversations job seekers initiate while networking. It may require multiple attempts and discussions before some contacts and employers feel comfortable talking freely. Therefore, in these instances job seekers need assert themselves and persist. Recall, from step four, *Planning*, that reputable em-

> *Closing*
> **Asking contacts • Employers**
> For information • Commitments •
> Decisions

ployers seek employees who possess productive-worker qualities or dynamic *self-management skills*. Among these traits are 'assertive' and 'persistent.'

KEEPING LINKED TO CONTACTS AND EMPLOYERS

Ongoing communication with contacts and employers, or **follow
up**, enables job seekers to build rapport. Both *corresponding* and *phone
calling* provide opportunities to confirm plans, repeat an earlier request,
review progress, remind, inform, update, and thank someone. First, we
look at how job seekers may correspond with contacts and employers.

To close contacts and employers successfully, helping facilitate your
progress, they may need
be reminded of your
background, qualifica-
tions, and objectives. Keep
them informed by writing
and sending notes, letters,
emails, telegrams or certified mail, resumes, and
'job-summary cards.'

Business cards dis-
tributed during the job
search are referred by

> *Build Rapport to Facilitate Progress*
> **Follow Up**
> Continued interaction
> Cultivates rapport
> **CORRESPONDING**
> Create links w/ Letters • Notes
> Resumes • Job-summary cards
> Email • Snail mail • Certified
> Telegrams • Hand-delivered
> **PHONE CALLING**
> Perform via telephone • Online
> Allows for verbal exchange

some as job-summary cards. Send or hand them (as you would when
employed) to individuals with whom you meet, speak, and/or interact: Those who can provide information, referrals, and, perhaps, hire
you. Attach to notes, letters, emails, resumes, and applications.

Preparing a Job-Summary Card

A **job-summary card** is a sketch of the job seeker's background,
qualifications, and objective utilized as a personal reminder, an an-
nouncement, or introduction. It may be saved as an electronic file
and printed on one side of an index or Rolodex® card.

Begin with a fresh electronic file and a blank card. Arrange the
information so text may be read in a few seconds. Include name,
phone number(s), e-mail address, position or career field you seek,
bare-bone self description, and noteworthy accomplishments and
skills. Format the data to fit neatly in an area 3"x5". For desktop
printing on blank, 3x5 index cards, select a reliable word-processing
application, such as MS Word.

A Job Seeker's Business Card

Job-Summary Card is a Personal Summary

Saved as electronic file
Printed on index• Rolodex® card
Read in seconds

Contains:

Name • Phone number(s) • E-mail address
Job objective • Career field
"Abridged" self description
Key accomplishments • Skills

Send • Hand to individuals

To Inform • Announce • Remind
w/ Resumes • Applications • Emails

On her computer, Mary Emerson opened a new electronic file. She wrote, designed, and saved a job-summary card. As a first 'quantity,' she printed on 3x5 Rolodex®cards, thirty hard copies. She sends one along with correspondence as a reminder of her background, qualifications, and objective. Also, she carries a few with her so she can hand one to individuals she meets in person. Compare her job-summary card to yours or use it as a guide to design your own.

• Mary Fashions a Job-Summary Card

MARY THERESA EMERSON

home: (301) 555-0100
mobile: (443) 555-0137
email: mtemerson@xyzmail.com

Seeking position in *Advertising/Media Sales*

3 years researching, creating, composing print & video projects. Write, edit, design art & copy. Computer literate. BA Communication Arts. Goucher Award recipient.

Member American Marketing Assn. Record of securing advertising clients. Analyzed & improved data-entry procedures w/ MS Excel program. Able to produce under pressure, i.e. met 25 consecutive deadlines.

Persistent, personable, results-oriented

C

Follow-up Correspondence

Correspond to keep connected with contacts and employers. When you do so, successfully, you reinforce a positive and professional image. Seize every opportunity to thank, update, and offer help to each individual with whom you interact. Also, convey intent to remain in touch. When appropriate, include or attach a job-summary card.

Utilize a *daily schedule* (hard copy or electronic) to prompt your correspondence. Enter the name of each contact or employer as a reminder or 'to do' item on the day you plan to write to her/him. (Step four; *Planning*, Mary's Daily Schedule). Consider these times and circumstances for follow-up correspondence:

- *Following each initial interaction.* To build a network of contacts and employers, job seekers often start by introducing themselves during an in-person conversation, a chat on the phone, or an online exchange.

  Within forty-eight hours after each opening conversation, chat, or exchange; send a note, brief letter, or an email.

- *Shortly before interviews.* Three or four days in advance, send a brief letter or email to confirm the time of the meeting.

- *Shortly after interviews and phone conversations (post-initial).* In a letter, summarize the dialogue from the latest conversation. State your thanks, promote yourself, and review plans. Send within the next two days.

- *To formally introduce phone calls.* You may have attempted three or four times to reach, on the phone, a contact or employer, and failed each time. Express in a note or letter, your desire to get her/his opinion. Begin with a compliment. Relate that you've attempted to reach her/him a number of times. Mention that you plan to call again.

  Refer to a particular day in the morning or afternoon, i.e. Monday afternoon. Insert into and address an envelope. Affix or write her/his name, company name, number and street, city, state and zip code. Make sure spelling is correct. Stamp and send via snail mail.

- *When an interview results in rejection, follow up.* Send a letter to thank the employer for the opportunity, and, announce that you plan to call. Then, call to ask the employer to reconsider his/her decision. (Occasionally, the employment picture changes and you may deal yourself back into consideration. See, Mary Follows Correspondence with a Phone Call, p.178)

- *To highlight career-shaping events.* Notify employers in writing, when you decline or accept a job offer, or terminate employment. Announce to friends, associates, and others; when you achieve a noteworthy accomplishment such as starting a new job.

> *Write to Refresh Others' Impressions of You*
> **Send notes • Letters • Emails**
> Projects a business image • Conveys good will
> Keeps job seekers linked w/ contacts • Employers
> **Appropriate before • After**
> Calls • Chats • Interviews • Offers
> To Accept • Decline • End employment

• Preparing Notes and Letters

Prospective employers and contacts judge job seekers by the appearance and content of correspondence. Keep notes, letters, and emails:

Direct. Use frank, simple language.

Positive. Upbeat messages only.

Brief. Use one side of one page. Keep sentences and paragraphs (maximum is four) short.

Correct. Check spelling, grammar, and punctuation.

Neat. Use stationery appropriate for business communication, and a quality printer for letters. If handwriting, write notes legibly.

Personal. Distinguish yourself. Describe something you've in common with the addressee or specific to your previous interaction.

> *Guidelines for Correspondence*
> **Demonstrates fundamental skills**
> Keep it direct • Positive • Brief
> Correct • Neat • Personal

For instance, mention the name(s) of (a) person(s) whom you both know, and/or an interest you share.

Mary sent a note and *job-summary card* to her new *contact*, Dick Metcalf, the day after initiating a conversation with him about her job search (step three, *Prospecting*, Mary's Network-Presentation Script). She opens by thanking Dick for his time and suggestion. She updates him referring to her job-summary card. Then, she conveys intent to remain in touch; encouraging him to be mindful of her and share his thoughts on her job search. Mary personalizes the note by naming the people Dick referred during their conversation.

• Mary Emerson's Note of Thanks to Contacts

From the desk of…

Mary Theresa Emerson

4/10/20--

Dear Dick,

Thank you for taking time from your busy schedule yesterday afternoon to chat with me. I appreciate your suggestion that I speak with Bob Gerber and Kitty Weldon. I plan to contact both during the next few days.

Enclosed, find my job-summary card. Please, share your thoughts concerning my job search. Feel free to call or email me.

Sincerely,
Mary Emerson

The next few pages depict letters Mary wrote to follow up with contacts and employers during her job search. These illustrate how she remains linked with them and helps facilitate her progress.

• More of Mary's Correspondence

Mary persuaded Ron Myers of Finch Advertising to interview her, upon making a successful *employer-telephone presentation*. Later, the same day, she wrote to confirm their plans to meet. She personalizes this letter by referring to comments Ron made during their phone conversation. The following day, she mailed it to him (pg. 170).

In step three, *Prospecting*, we reviewed Mary's conversation with Jim Everett, an *industry contact* (Mary's Industry-Contact Presentation Script). The result of this conversation, Jim referred to Mary, Ralph DiPietro; the Director of sales at Cobson Industries. When she phoned and spoke with Ralph, he invited her to meet.

Mary Builds Rapport with Letters
Writing to Contacts and Employers, She:
Confirms plans • Expresses thanks
Promotes herself • Summarizes interaction
Accepts a job offer • Updates others

After their interview, Mary composed a letter. She begins by thanking him. She mentions Dipietro's plans about which she learned in the interview, thus, personalizing it. She promotes herself, emphasizing she'd jump at the opportunity to work for Cobson; recaps her qualifications; and, suggests she could generate sales quickly (an employer benefit). In the final paragraph, Mary confirms their plans repeating the commitment Ralph made during the interview. Here, she refers to Dipietro's proposition to bring her back for a second look. She attached the letter to an email two days after the interview (pg. 171).

After evaluating the proposal from Bob Stiles of Publican Industries (step six, *Negotiating*), Mary wrote a letter of acceptance. She then wrote to each person who provided information, ideas and referrals during her job search. She updates them about her new job, and where they may now reach her. After extending gratitude, she expresses intent to remain in touch (pg. 172).

To track and confirm to whom she has sent correspondence, Mary makes a record of each note, letter, email, and job-summary card (J-SC) in a *Correspondence Log* (pg. 173).

• Mary Emerson's Letter of Confirmation

MARY THERESA EMERSON
6408 Brampton Place
Wheaton, MD 20902
(home) 301-555-0100 • (mobile) 443-555-0137
(email) *mtemerson@xyzmail.com*

April 5, 20--

Mr. Ronald M. Myers
District Sales Manager
FINCH ADVERTISING, INC.
1302 Rockville Pike
Rockville, MD 20854

Dear Ron:

I enjoyed our phone conversation earlier today. The Lipman project you described sounds fascinating. Thanks for taking time to talk about it. I hope you get a portion, if not all, of it.

I look forward to our meeting Friday afternoon, the 8th, to discuss your suburban Maryland-DC territory. I plan to be at your office at 3 p.m. sharp. If there are any changes, please contact me before then.

Sincerely,

Mary Emerson

Mary Emerson

• Mary's Letter Following Interview

MARY THERESA EMERSON
6408 Brampton Place
Wheaton, MD 20902
(home) 301-555-0100 • (mobile) 443-555-0137
(email) *mtemerson@xyzmail.com*

April 8, 20--

Mr. Ralph Dipietro
Director of Sales
COBSON INDUSTRIES, INC.
5397 Indiana Avenue
Alexandria, VA 22312

Dear Mr. Dipietro:

I enjoyed meeting you yesterday and learning about Cobson Industries. Thank you for taking the time to interview with me.

The interview confirmed my initial impression that Cobson is a progressive company. Your plans to expand in-house, desktop publishing services interest me. You gave me confidence that Cobson's share of the available market for customized promotions will grow.

Though I desire to learn more, I believe I'd jump at the opportunity to come work for you. My experience with computers, advertising design and layout, department directors and budgets; my passion for art; degree in Communications; and, desire to develop and polish my selling skills, will enable me to generate new sales. Thus, I'm convinced I can quickly become a productive member of Cobson Industries' sales team.

Please call or email me if plans change and require rescheduling. Otherwise, I look forward to spending next Thursday in the field with Allison Sheppard, your rep in the DC area.

Sincerely,

Mary Emerson

Mary Emerson

• Mary Informs Those in Her Network of Her Success

PUBLICAN INDUSTRIES, INC.
1032 Whitesford Place
Silver Spring, MD 20910
(voice) 301-555-0147 • (fax) 301-555-0187
www.publicanind.com

June 4, 20--

Mr. Richard Metcalf
1216 Valley Way
Potomac, MD 20854

Dear Dick:

I'm pleased to inform you of my association with Publican Industries in Silver Spring, Maryland. I started working as their new Advertising Representative for the D.C. area on the first of the month. Enclosed, please find a business card.

I seize this opportunity to extend my appreciation for your generous consideration, thoughtful advice, and helpful referrals. With your contribution to my job search, I was able to accomplish my mission.

Please feel free to refer to me individuals you know who utilize professional-quality advertising. We offer a complete line of print and video services. I'll be in touch with you soon. Again, thank you.

With much admiration,

Mary Emerson

Mary Emerson

• Mary Emerson's Correspondence Log

Contact	Company	Purpose	Date
Dick Metcalf	(home)	Thanks-note/J-SC	3/25/ - -
Ron Myers	Finch Advertising	Confirm appointment	4/08/ - -
Ralph Dipietro	Cobson Industries	Follow-up interview	4/08/ - -
Ray Golson	Golson Advertising	Reply to rejection/J-SC	4/09/ - -
Sharon Gillespie	Rotaine Enterprises	Decline offer	4/09/ - -
Bob Stiles	Publican Industries	Accept offer	5/15/ - -
Dick Metcalf	(home)	Update/Thanks	6/04/ - -

Next, let's see how phone calls keep job seekers linked to contacts and employers.

PRIMARY TOOL: THE PHONE

The *follow-up phone call*, simply, calling back after having initiated interaction, is a highly-effective way to get a job.[43] Via follow-up phone calls or presentations, job seekers re-connect with contacts and employers. To speak, again, directly with them, enables job seekers to extend and develop the dialogue. Hence, they may express interest with sincerity, obtain details and commitments, resolve problems, clarify and magnify prior communications, discover opportunities, and get results quickly.

You may prefer email or even to exchange text messages in place of, or in addition to, phone calls. This author recommends the telephone as your primary tool for follow up. It permits you (the 'caller') to incorporate into the dialogue the receiver's expressions (i.e. tone or inflection of message, pace or rhythm, directness, level of excitement, cues related to stress) and responses in real time. Thus, phone calls, which provide for exchange of spoken messages, deliver greater meaning. Use other forms of communication as a supplement to follow-up phone presentations. (Revisit step four, *Planning*, ETP.)

Once a link with a contact or an employer is established, call back to get information, decisions, secure commitments and, consequently, build rapport. Consider these times and circumstances for a follow-up call:

- *After sending notes, letters, etc.* Call three to eight days after you place correspondence in the mail.

- *To complete a diverted attempt.* Some people may cut short or stifle your attempt to initiate interaction. For instance, say you introduce yourself, on the phone, to a referral who reacts as if s/he is unable or unwilling to chat. Politely express regrets. After a few days, try again.

  Say you request something of a contact or employer who replies, "I'll call you back." If two or three days go by, and s/he fails to call back; call again to repeat your request.

- *To reverse a rejection.* A few days after an employer-telephone presentation (if unsuccessful), call employers again to improve your appeal with a more-carefully prepared message for a meeting. (Often, polite persistence pays off!)

- *After making plans.* Suppose an employer invites you for a meeting. An hour or two before the time of such meeting, call to confirm.

- *After an interview that concludes without a commitment.* Call the employer, the next day or two, to request a commitment or learn why s/he has hesitated.

> *Follow-Up Calls Advance Interaction*
> **Utilize telephone to get results quickly**
> Call employers • Contacts • After initial interaction
> To extend dialogue • Build rapport
> **Identify • Resolve:**
> Problems • Concerns • Misunderstandings
> Reverse failed ETP
> Keep in touch w/ those in network • Convey interest
> Update • Repeat requests • Get info • Hold others to pledges
> Confirm interviews • Plans • Clarify • Obtain commitments

Preparing the Follow-Up Call

Allot, on your *daily schedule,* time each day for making follow-up phone calls. Before each call, however, determine what you want to accomplish! Some calls require more preparation than others. Utilize a *chat log* (hard copy or electronic) to project, arrange, and list follow-up calls. Enter the *date, name, title, company, phone number, e-address* and *source of name* for each contact or employer. (See, Mary Logs Completed Calls, pg 181). As you would the network, industry-contact, and employ-

> ### Before Follow-Up Calls
> **Pre-determine aim of call**
> Notate 'to do' items on Daily Schedule
> Enter data onto Chat Log
> **Script your part in 4 steps**
> Attention-Grabber • Identify
> Payoff • Signoff

er-telephone presentations; to make productive follow-up phone presentations, script your part and apply the basic *four-step formula*: *Attention-Grabber*, *Identify*, *Payoff*, and *Signoff*. (Part two, Companion, *Follow-Up Call Guide*.)

In step one, *Attention-Grabber*, greet the callee and state your name. Demonstrate courtesy; state the reason for your call, then ask for his/her time. I.e. "I'm calling because...Do you have a few minutes to chat?"

Step two, *Identify*. Extend or develop the dialogue. Remind the callee of your prior interaction or exchange. Describe briefly what's happened since then. Ask the employer or contact for details, commitments, names, clarifications, or to reconsider something. For example, you may say, "Let me ask again that you grant me a face-to-face meeting. I wish to learn more about you and ABC Company. I've a more compelling reason for you to revisit the issue with me. Okay?"

In step three, *Payoff*. Make clear what it is that you want this person to do or say. Ask questions (you've prepared and placed on your script) or, share with the callee previously-prepared responses and rebuttals. Determine the next step. Ask the contact or employer, "What's next?"

In step four, *Signoff*, confirm phone numbers, addresses, and the purpose for continuing to communicate. Repeat the plans derived from your conversation with the employer or contact and offer thanks for her/his time and interest.

The next three illustrations are scripts Mary Emerson prepared to guide her follow-up phone conversations.

Mary called Bill Jackson, an *industry contact* employed with Phazur Enterprises, to obtain his opinion. Bill needed time to think about Mary's request for a recommendation. He told Mary he would return her call. After three days without hearing from Bill, Mary called him back to repeat her request.

• Mary Repeats a Request

Attention-Grabber

Good morning, Bill. This is Mary Emerson.

I wish to continue our conversation from Monday afternoon.

Are you able to take a minute to shed some light on our industry?

Identify

You may recall I requested advice about the advertising industry. You were occupied, however; you said you'd give some thought to some recommendations for me.

After giving this some thought, are you able to refer someone knowledgeable about this industry who may chat with me?

Payoff

I understand why you feel that way. Of course, I'll keep your recommendations confidential if you wish.

Who do you know who's largely respected in the industry? Tell me about them. Thanks. Tell me about you, Bill. How long have you been with Phazur? What exactly does Phazur do? What do you do for them?....

Signoff

I'd like to keep you informed of my progress. Okay?

Here's my phone number and email. (443) 555-0137 and mtemerson@xyzmail.com.

May I email you? What's your address?

For sharing a bit about yourself, Phazur, and the referrals -- thank you, Bill.

Mistakenly, some job seekers conclude job interviews without expressing desire to have the job, and, thus, without a *commitment*. In the event you leave an interview without a commitment from the employer, follow up with a phone call. Though less effective than during the interview, it provides an opportunity to interact, again, with the employer and obtain a commitment. Mary left her interview with Ron Myers at Finch Advertising failing to ask for the job, and, thus, without a commitment. After realizing this, the next morning, she made a follow-up phone presentation.

• Mary Secures a Commitment

Attention-Grabber

Good morning, Ron. This is Mary Emerson.

You may know why I'm calling. I left our interview without completing my business with you.

Can you spend a minute?

Identify

Let me take this opportunity to thank you, again, for the interview. You may recall, I left after you asked if I had any more questions. As a result of my research, our interview and thoughtful consideration, I'm most interested to come work for you at Finch Advertising. I want the job, Ron.

What are your feelings on this matter? Do you have any concerns at this time?

Payoff

If any questions or concerns arise, please share them with me. I want to make sure you've the information you need to be confident that hiring me is the right decision.

What, then is the next step?

Signoff

You have my number and email, right?

I'll see you, then,... (on Friday at three).

Thanks Ron, I feel a whole lot better.

Interviewed and rejected by Golson Advertising, Mary sent a letter and job-summary card to Ray Golson. In the letter, she alerted him to expect a phone call. After a few days, she acted on this opportunity to persuade Golson to change his mind. She prepared the following script to guide her conversation.

• Mary Follows Correspondence with a Phone Call

Attention-Grabber

Good morning, Mr. Golson. This is Mary Emerson.

I'm calling to inquire about your progress regarding the sales position we discussed last Monday, the 24th.

Can you spend a minute?

Identify

I received your letter. Thanks. Did you get mine?

Might there still be an opportunity for me to come to work for you? Has the person whom is your first choice accepted your offer? Would you kindly share the reason why I was rejected? Let me make certain I understand. I was rejected because.... Is that right? Are there any other reasons? Am I qualified for this position? If it resulted in more things getting done, less waste, and elevated team spirit; Would you replace a mediocre employee with someone who's more energetic, productive, and enthusiastic?

Payoff

Mr. Golson, I respect your right to select the person you see as the best fit. Also, I understand decisions like this may be challenging. Tell me, what may I say to win your confidence that I'm the one for this job? When should I follow up for the purpose of becoming a productive member of your sales team?

Signoff

I welcome your thoughts and ideas concerning my job search. I'll get back with you...

May I restate for you my phone number and email? (443) 555-0137 and mtemerson@xyzmail.com.

Once again, thank you Mr. Golson; for the interview, your interest, and consideration.

More Ways to Follow Up

In addition to corresponding and phone calling, there are more ways to follow up. You might visit spontaneously with contacts and employers, or recruit a 'representative.'

By way of an unannounced visit, you can make a favorable impression. Though business people at work may be uncomfortable about unexpected interruptions, some will talk with you when polite and to the point.

> *Use Imagination
> to Keep Interaction Productive*
> **Make an Unannounced Visit**
> Be polite
> May result in favorable impression
> **Have Representative Participate**
> S/he to tell others about you
> Sway others to talk w/you

Occasionally, your efforts may meet resistance. Should you find yourself staring at an apparent impasse, people who know you can provide follow up. Stay in command, however. At your request, on your terms, instruct them to inform, inquire, and/or update others about you. For example, say you interviewed two days ago with a reputable company in which you're very interested. The employer has yet to make a commitment. You call twice, then, a third time to get an update. Mysteriously the employer is unavailable. Among your *network* of *contacts*, identify someone who knows the employer. Ideally, your *references* fit the bill.

Upon speaking with the employer on your behalf, this representative may be able to obtain relevant information, thus, defining more clearly, your status. This could give you the edge to secure a commitment.

Say you've spoken twice with an employer to arrange an interview, and both times s/he denied you an opportunity. Here, again, enlist a representative. As before select a contact; one who knows you well and may know the employer. Instruct the contact, so s/he politely encourages the employer to meet with you.

Notating Follow-Up Activities

In step two of Gopp, Inc.™ *Organizing*, we set up *logs*, *member profiles*, and/or suitable electronic files, to store notes. These become records of conversations, correspondence, and noteworthy data enabling job seekers to measure progress.

On an index card, and/or in an electronic file, describe briefly each communication with, and key information about each contact and employer. Kept current, these notes and summaries chronicle progress and prompt you for future follow up. Entries for follow-up activities may denote *correspondence*, *phone calls*, *online exchanges*, *visits*, and, upon your instruction, *interaction provided by representatives.*

Below, Mary summarizes her interaction with employees of Finch Advertising in an electronic-network file and creates a manual back up on the back of an index card. Ron Myers, the sales manager for Finch, is referred to Mary by Kitty Weldon, one of her contacts.

> ### After Performing Follow-Up Activities
>
> **Make notes on index cards**
> **Electronic file**
>
> Correspondence • Phone calls
> Online exchanges • Visits
> Contributions from representatives
> Instructions for further follow up

Mary discovers Finch during a visit to the Chamber of Commerce and starts a *member profile* on an index card (3/23). She identifies Myers as an employer who may have an opening (3/30). She attempts an *employer-telephone presentation* (3/31). She notes her presentation to the sales manager (4/3). On 4/4, she sends a letter confirming their plans to meet (a follow-up activity). On 4/8, she calls prior to the appointment to confirm (again, a follow-up activity).

As part of her daily activities, Mary also makes entries and checks off completed calls in a *chat log* (see below).

• Mary Summarizes Follow-Up Activities

(Front)

Finch Advertising, Inc.	2	301-555-0161
1302 Rockville Pike		*www.finchadv.com*
Rockville, Maryland 20854		
	Ron Myers--District SM--ext.57	
	Cheryl Madison -- Sec.	
Specialize in print advertising: trade journals		

(Back)

3/23/--	Member of Chamber of Commerce. Saw ad they did for 'Biotech Engineering' displayed at the Chamber.
3/30/--	Kitty Weldon of Mehcom knows Ron. Says he's always looking for talented people.
3/31/--	Left name w/ Cheryl. Try calling back Monday.
4/3/--	ETP to Ron. Got interview. Set for Friday, the 8th, 3 p.m.
4/4/--	Sent confirmation letter. (Copy in file)
4/8/--	Spoke w/ Cheryl. Confirmed appointment w/ Ron. It's on!

• Mary Logs Completed Calls

DAY: *Monday*   DATE: *04/09/20--*

GOALS

Presentations	Number Projected	Completed
Network	2	☑
Industry-contact	2	☑
Employer-telephone	1	☑
Follow-up	3	☑

CALLS/EXCHANGES

Contact	Title	Company	Phone	E-Address	Referred By
Don Graber	Pastor	St. Mary's Church	301 555-0145	dgraber@xyzmail.com	(@ church)
Ross Miller	Branch Mgr.	Wells Forge bank	301 555-0141	rmiller1@anyco.net	(@ bank)
Joe Yost	Sales Mgr.	Minute Press	410 555-0110	jyost@xyzmail.com	Uncle Jim
Sue Weyforth	Dir. Design	Raleegh Ent.	410 555-0198	sweyforth@acom.org	Aunt Betty

John Reese	Sales Dir.	AVCO Creations	301 555-0160	jreese@anyco.net	Judy Larson (@CGA)
Bill Jackson	Media Rep.	Phazur Ent.	301 555-0124	bjackson@anyco.net	Don Lasalle (@spa)
Ron Myers	District Mgr.	Finch Adv.	301-555-0153	rmyers@xyzmail.com	Kitty Weldon
Ray Golson	Owner/ Pres.	Golson Adv.	703 555-0195	rgolson@xyzmail.com	Gail White (@ Chamber of Commerce)

SUMMARY

In the course of conducting their everyday affairs, business people ask others for opinions, agreement, permission, or approval. Some refer to this act as "*closing.*" Individuals in search of meaningful employment need 'close' knowledgeable and influential persons who may help facilitate their progress. Often, however, they must first establish rapport. Careful *follow up* or ongoing communication keeps job seekers linked to contacts and employers, enabling them to gain favor. Consequently, contacts and employers share with job seekers useful information, favorable decisions, and helpful commitments; all of which are necessary for acquiring a meaningful job.

Here are four ways to follow up: *correspondence, phone calls, visits,* and *representatives.* All may be accomplished under the charge of the job seeker. Utilize a *daily schedule,* listing each follow-up activity as a 'to do' item to be performed on a specific day. Your list becomes a guide as you endeavor each day to carry out the intended actions.

Prepare and send *correspondence* to thank, remind, inform, update, confirm plans, repeat earlier requests, and review progress. It keeps you linked to others. Within forty-eight hours after each opening conversation, chat, or exchange; send a note, brief letter, or an email. Three or four days in advance of a scheduled meeting, send a letter to confirm. Send a letter to announce to others that you'll be calling them on the phone to seek their opinion. A day after an interview, send a letter and, perhaps, a *job-summary card* to thank the employer, review plans, and reinforce your candidacy. Send correspondence to highlight a significant event.

Make *follow-up phone calls*, or call back individuals who may help facilitate your progress. These phone conversations re-connect job seekers with contacts and employers enabling them to get results quickly. Begin by preparing a script to follow so calls are purposeful and productive. Call three to eight days after sending correspondence to confirm plans, get decisions, and secure commitments. To obtain information, check back in two or three days when someone fails to return your call. Call a few days after an employer-telephone presentation (if unsuccessful) to clarify communications with a more-carefully prepared message and to repeat your request for a meeting. Every time an appointment is scheduled, call an hour or two before, to confirm. Should an interview conclude without a *commitment*, call the employer the next day to request one, learn why s/he has hesitated, and; if necessary, resolve problems.

To supplement correspondence and follow-up phone calls, make *unannounced visits* to employers and others located nearby who may receive you. If stymied, instruct *representatives* when they can deliver results which may help facilitate your progress. Write notes on index cards (*member profiles*) and/or make entries in an electronic file to chronicle each attempt to interact, summarize every communication, and prompt your next move. Upon sending notes, letters, emails, telegrams, certified mail, job-summary cards and resumes; note and/or make entries in a *correspondence log* to keep track and confirm correspondence. Keep records of follow-up calls (presentations) and online exchanges in a *chat log*. By following up, job seekers establish rapport; strengthening relationships with contacts and employers. Once comfortable, they may freely share with job seekers information, decisions, and commitments.

As job seekers communicate with others in a productive manner, advancing their progress and realizing gainful results such as viable *leads*, challenging *interviews*, and appealing *job offers*; they bring within reach their destination -- a meaningful position with a reputable employer!

This concludes step seven, *Closing*, and, thus, your project for Gopp, Inc.™ As you sign an ideal employment proposal and begin your new job, the SDJS is complete. You've traveled the road of responsibility and initiative safely to success. Congratulations! Thank you for utilizing *Sure Hire Made Easy*.

NOTES

Introduction

1. U.S. Department of Labor, Bureau of Labor Statistics, *Bulletin 1886*. See: Education Resources Information Center, ed117476, *Jobseeking Methods Used By American Workers*, http://www.eric.ed.gov/.

2. Dawson and Dawson Management Consultants, *Job Search: The Total System*, 1988, p.82. See also, 3rd edition 11/1/2008.

3. Bolles, Richard N., *What Color is Your Parachute*, 1989, ppg.18-19. Farr, J. Michael, *Getting the Job You Really Want*, 1988, p.40.

4. Lathrop, Richard, *The Job Market*, 1978.

5. Bolles, Richard N., *Parachute*, 1989, p.14. Breaugh, James, *Academy of Management Journal*, #24, 3/81, ppg. 142-147. Kaufman, H.G., *Professionals in Search of Work*, 1982.

6. Beatty, Richard H., *Get The Right Job in 60 Days or Less*, 1991, ppg.47-48.

7. Bowman, William, *How College Graduates Find Good Jobs*, based on Maryland State Board of Higher Education, *Journal of Career Planning and Employment*, #48, winter, 1987, ppg. 32-36.

8. U.S. Bureau of Census, *Current Population Survey*, 1973. Robert S. Gardella, *The Harvard Business School Guide To Finding Your Next Job*, 2000, ppg. 90-93.

9. Farr, Gaither, Pickrell, *The Work Book*, 1987, p. 122.

10. U.S. Department of Labor, Bureau of Labor Statistics, *Current Population Survey*, www.bls.gov/cps/labor2006/, chart 2-1

11. Hudson Institute. http://www.hudson.org/index.cfm?fuseaction

12. U.S. Department of Labor, Bureau of Labor Statistics, *Employment Outlook: 2006–16*, http://www.bls.gov/opub/mlr/2007/11/art3full.pdf

13. U.S. Department of Labor, Bureau of Labor Statistics. *Current Population Survey*, Annual Averages - Household Data, http://www.bls.gov/cps/cpsaat31.pdf, see also:

http://www.bls.gov/cps/tables.htm entry numbers 30, A-35, D-18.

14. U.S. Department of Labor, Bureau of Labor Statistics; *Monthly Labor Review*, Nov. 2007. http://www.bls.gov/emp/empmajorindout.htm

15. Ibid. http://www.bls.gov/emp/empfastestind.htm

16. Ibid. http://www.bls.gov/emp/emptab3.htm. Table 3. See also: http://www.bls.gov/cps/labor2006/chart1-19.pdf

17. U.S. Department of Labor, *Report On The American Workforce*, 2001, p.2. Bulletin 2174, *Jobs: A Chartbook on Unemployment*, July 1983. Bulletin 2096, *Labor Force Statistics Derived Front the Current Population Survey : A Datebook*, September 1982. www.bls.gov/opub/mlr/1984/06/art2full.pdf

18. Rodgers, Johnson, Alexander, *Secrets of the Hidden Job Market*, 1986, p.8. Walsh, Johnson, Sugerman, *Case Studies of Classified Ads*, 1975.

19. Farr, J. Michael, *Job Finding Fast*, 1990, p.11.

20. Magnum, Stephen, *Job Search: A Review of the Literature*, 1982. Lunsden and Sharf, *Behavioral Dimensions of the Job Interview*, Journal of College Placement, spring, 1974. Rosenfeld, Carl, *Job Search of the Unemployed*, Monthly Labor Review, Vol 100, 11/77, ppg.39-43. Lathrop, Richard, *The Job Market*, 1978.

21. Granovetter, Mark S., *Getting a Job: A Study of Contacts and Careers*, 1974. Wegmann, Chapman, Johnson, *Work in the New Economy*, 1989, p. 145. U.S. Department of Labor, Bureau of Labor Statistics, *Bulletin 1886,* See: Education Resources Information Center, ed117476, *Jobseeking Methods....*, http://www.eric.ed.gov/.

22. Lathrop, Richard, *The Job Market*, 1978.

Goal Setting

23. http://bookstore.gpo.gov/actions/GetPublication.do?stocknumber=029-001-03478-4

24. O*NET OnLine, see: http://www.onetcodeconnector.org/ http://www.doleta.gov/programs/onet. See also; the Developer's Corner at http://www.doleta.gov/leave-oleta.cfm?target=http://www.onetcenter.org

25. http://bookstore.gpo.gov/actions/GeneralSearch.do, search under Occupational Outlook Handbook.

26. http://www.pearsonassessments.com/cdmr.aspx, see; level two. See also; http://www.eric.ed.gov/ERICWebPortal/custom/portlets/recordDetails/

detailmini.jsp?_nfpb=true&_&ERICExtSearch_SearchValue_0=EJ669347&ERICExtSearch_SearchType_0=no&accno=EJ669347

Prospecting

27. http://www.loc.gov/rr/business/duns/duns23.html

28. http://www.dnbmdd.com/mddi/

29. http://www.Mergentonline.com

30. http://www.netadvantage.standardandpoors.com/NetAd/demo/home.htm

31. http://www.thomasnet.com/companyhistory/ThomasRegister_today.html

    See, also: http://www.thomasnet.com/

32. http://www.census.gov/eos/www/naics/

33. Farr, J. Michael, *Getting the Job You Really Want*, 1988, p.48.

Planning

34. Endicott study. Lundsen and Sharf, *Behavioral Dimensions of the Job* Interview.

35. Schiffman, *Power Sales Presentations*, ppg.62-64. Shook, Shafiroff,

    Successful Telephone Selling in the 80's, p.13.

36. Farr, J. *Michael, Getting the Job You Really Want*, p.73.

37. Bruno, Tony, *The Bruno System for Success*, p.28.

Interviewing

38. Pettus, T., *One on One*, p.95.

39. Krannich, *Careering and Recareering for the 1990's*, p.206.

40. Whiting, *The 5 Great Rules of Selling*, p.113.

Negotiating

41. http://data.bls.gov/oes/search.jsp?data_tool=OES

    www.bls.gov/cps/tables.htm, www.data.bls.gov/oes/datatype.do,

    www.salary.com

42. Allen, Jeffrey G., *How To Turn An Interview Into A Job*, p.73.

Closing

43. Farr, J. *Michael, Getting the Job You Really Want*, 1988, p.124, ex:3.

DIAGRAMS

JOB-SEARCH PATHWAYS

Job seekers utilize various strategies to conduct a job search. Most commonly, they rely upon others to act on their behalf to advance their progress. Then, there are those less-popular approaches where job seekers take charge; assuming the action. Thus, these are performed under the control of the job seeker.

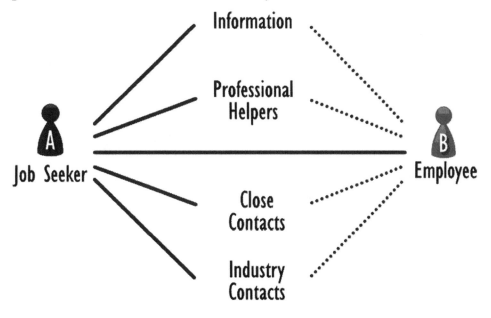

Key:	
▬▬▬▬▬	Job Seeker assumes action, thus able to effect progress
●●●●●●●●●●●	Job Seeker entrusts others to effect progress, thus, relinquishes control.
Information	*advertisements, applications, job fairs, lists profiles, resumes*
Professional Helpers	*personnel services, employment agencies, public assistance centers, career and placement counselors, job-search consultants, recruiters, etc.*
Close Contacts	*friends, family members, acquaintances*
Industry Contacts	*individuals associated with career field or industry*

JOB-SEARCH BRIDGE

Sections

Success at job searching begins with a simple concept: a bridge. When built properly, it safely joins points A (job seeker) and B (employee). This approach brings the job-search journey under the control (under the 'feet') of the job seeker. Thus, job seekers may merely 'walk' across to Point B.

Most bridges require *footers*; vertical columns upon which the structure rests, a *superstructure*; an upward extension above the peak line of the columns over which the deck is built, and a *deck*; or roadbed, which is the roadway, pedestrian walkway, or the horizontal surface.

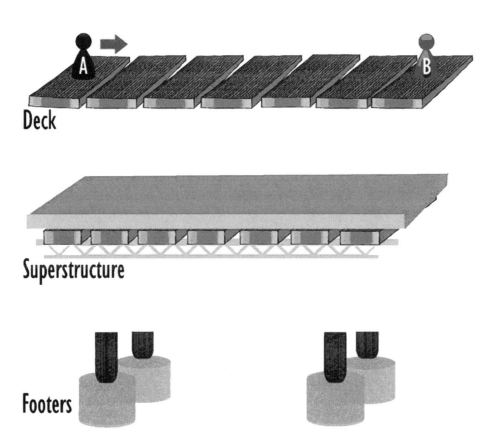

Deck

Superstructure

Footers

JOB-SEARCH BRIDGE

Components

To build a 'job-search bridge' requires footers; fundamental communication skills and activities upon which the job search develops. A superstructure comprising advanced-level skills and abilities necessary for supporting the 'surface' and, thus, a successful search. And, a deck; the activities cited most often as action parts, or, the 'pathway,' of a job search.

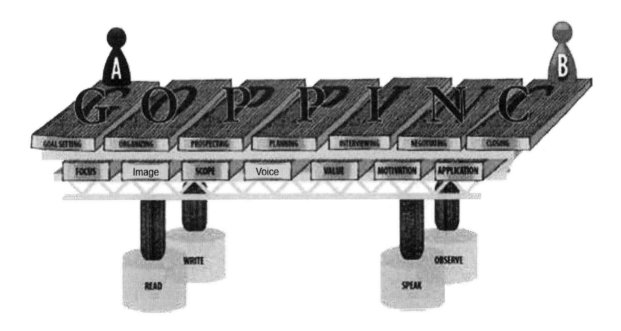

INDEX